"This beautifully written study is a celebration of a particular church committed to help a dislocated college-educated generation make sense of its own changing world and in the process restore African society to wholeness. The issues raised and the way they are discussed contribute greatly to understanding the current dynamics within African Christianity."

Paul Gifford, emeritus professor, SOAS, University of London

"This is *not* yet another book on African Pentecostalism. Rather it is a highly original study of a Kenyan megachurch whose roots lie in conservative evangelical traditions of a very different kind. The Victorian mission theorist Henry Venn dreamed of establishing autonomous churches supported by a prosperous middle class, able to take their own mission initiatives throughout the continent. Wanjiru Gitau's engaging account shows how Nairobi's Mavuno Church has remarkably fulfilled those dreams among the millennial generation in Africa."

Brian Stanley, professor of world Christianity, University of Edinburgh

"It is now old news that the demographic center of Christianity has moved to the Majority World. This unusually insightful book goes well beyond the old news to explain how Mavuno Church in Nairobi, Kenya, became a thriving megachurch in a very short time. Besides an awful lot of fascinating ground-up information, *Megachurch Christianity Reconsidered* is also rich in cultural insight and social-political wisdom. The book is even more important for its deep theological testimony to the potential of holistic Christianity wherever it takes root."

Mark Noll, author of *The New Shape of World Christianity*

"Most studies about African Christianity focus on how the faith relates to traditional Africa or how it has dealt with colonialism. As Africa becomes more urban and globally interactive, however, so does African Christianity. Megachurches spring up in every metro area on the continent. Where do they come from? Why do they grow? What difference do they make? European and American scholars have argued that African megachurches merely mimic those in the Northern Hemisphere. Dr. Gitau makes it clear, however, that these new assemblies are genuinely African responses to their contexts. She combines an insider's knowledge of this movement with the analytic tools of theology and social science to create a lively, refreshing, and original account of urban African Christianity."

Joel Carpenter, Nagel Institute for the Study of World Christianity, Calvin College

"While plenty of works now speak generally of African Christianity, this book is such a treasure because of its specific detail, its rich and textured account of the growth of a thriving megachurch. This is a smart and thoughtful analysis of an extraordinarily important phenomenon in contemporary Christianity."

Philip Jenkins, distinguished professor of history, Baylor University

"This is a compelling narrative, analysis, and interpretation of the genesis and development of Nairobi's Mavuno Church, founded in 2005. Based on her first-hand experience in the congregation, case-study research, and postcolonial-missional analysis, Wanjiru Gitau offers a nuanced apologia for a young mega-church whose mission is to turn educated millennials into fearless influencers of Kenya, Africa, and the world. If Gitau is right, Mavuno's integration of dynamic contemporary worship, intensive catechesis and discipleship, and practical social engagement may prove to be a compelling vision for urban millennials beyond Kenya."

Thomas John Hastings, executive director, Overseas Ministries Study Center, and editor of *International Bulletin of Mission Research*

"I'm not sure there is any analysis out there quite like Wanjiru Gitau's *Megachurch Christianity Reconsidered*. Somehow Gitau has managed a wide-ranging, global, and multidisciplinary study that stays anchored in the running example of Mavuno Church and its leaders. This study respects historical backgrounds, all the while addressing the contemporary realities of millennials, 'Afropolitans,' and Africa's 'youth bulge.' Gitau has done us all a tremendous service by concretely and adeptly explaining how God is working among worldwide megachurch formations today, as well as leading such movements into tomorrow. Don't miss this unique and groundbreaking story."

J. Nelson Jennings, mission pastor, consultant, international liaison at Onnuri Church

MEGACHURCH CHRISTIANITY RECONSIDERED

Millennials and Social Change in African Perspective

WANJIRU M. GITAU

Foreword by Mark R. Shaw

IVP Academic

An imprint of InterVarsity Press
Downers Grove, Illinois

InterVarsity Press
P.O. Box 1400, Downers Grove, IL 60515-1426
ivpress.com
email@ivpress.com

InterVarsity Press® is the book-publishing division of InterVarsity Christian Fellowship/USA®, a movement of students and faculty active on campus at hundreds of universities, colleges, and schools of nursing in the United States of America, and a member movement of the International Fellowship of Evangelical Students. For information about local and regional activities, visit intervarsity.org.

Cover design: David Fassett
Interior design: Beth McGill
Image: © Mavuno, all rights reserved. Fearless Summit 2015. Courtesy of Mavuno Church.

ISBN 978-0-8308-5103-4 (print)
ISBN 978-0-8308-7374-6 (digital)

Printed in the United States of America ♾

InterVarsity Press is committed to ecological stewardship and to the conservation of natural resources in all our operations. This book was printed using sustainably sourced paper.

Library of Congress Cataloging-in-Publication Data

Names: Gitau, Wanjiru M., 1977- author.
Title: Megachurch Christianity reconsidered : millennials and social change
   in African perspective / Wanjiru M. Gitau.
Description: Downers Grove : InterVarsity Press, 2018. | Series:
   Missiological engagements series | Includes index.
Identifiers: LCCN 2018022300 (print) | LCCN 2018033168 (ebook) | ISBN
   9780830873746 (eBook) | ISBN 9780830851034 (pbk. : alk. paper)
Subjects: LCSH: Big churches—Africa. | Generation Y—Religious life. |
   Social change—Africa. | Social change—Religious aspects—Christianity.
Classification: LCC BV637.9 (ebook) | LCC BV637.9 .G58 2018 (print) | DDC
   276.762/5083—dc23
LC record available at https://lccn.loc.gov/2018022300

P 25 24 23 22 21 20 19 18 17 16 15 14 13 12 11 10 9 8 7 6 5 4 3 2 1

Y 37 36 35 34 33 32 31 30 29 28 27 26 25 24 23 22 21 20 19 18

I dedicate this book
to my late mother, Jane Wangui wa Gitau,
a woman of extraordinary resilience despite life's challenges. May this
work vindicate your long and hard labor of love.

Contents

List of Figures

Foreword

Mark R. Shaw

As the title makes clear, this is a book about megachurches. It's a book that says many of the things that most books on megachurches say. You will find demographics, case studies, and good social science. But it is much more than this. This is a book about radical change and how it happens. It is a book that answers a question I have wondered about for the last several decades. What makes tens of millions of African young people stream to church every Sunday while an equal number of Western young people seem to be moving in the opposite direction?

Dr. Wanjiru Gitau tackles this question by taking us across the world to Nairobi, Kenya. There she tells the story of Mavuno, an African megachurch. Founded in 2005 with a few hundred people, Mavuno became one of Nairobi's fastest growing and most innovative megachurches. The author tells the important story of this spiritual skyscraper that has changed the religious and cultural skyline of Nairobi.

Let me mention three features of her story that captured me. First, this is a story about people. The author captures the world of East Africa in the late twentieth century. She then places her cast of characters onto this tumultuous stage. And interesting characters they are. Oscar Muriu graduates from seminary only to be assigned a dying church of twenty-five people. What happened next was not a funeral but a new birth. Oscar led a youth revival that changed the religious map of Nairobi. Muriithi Wanjau, acting as Melanchthon to Oscar's Luther, streamlined the movement and sent it on a global journey. A large supporting cast of sincere, talented, and committed young people streamed into the movement and carried it to new levels of cultural and global impact. All of this happened from below, with God using people like you and me. This is history with a human face.

We were reminded a few decades ago by the fall of the Berlin wall and the collapse of the Soviet Union that people are the great change agents in God's world, not just impersonal forces. Dr. Gitau captures this truth.

Secondly, this is a story about movements and how they work. Dr. Gitau approaches the megachurch story from a neglected angle: the perspective of history and the dynamics of people movements. She takes a few pages from the study of revival and revitalization movements around the world and judiciously uses these insights to probe the meaning of her story. Much is to be gained from the social scientific study of megachurches. Outstanding researchers have provided valuable service by mining the descriptive and contextual features of modern megachurches. But only history can show clearly how revival movements are the real origin story of the great megachurches around the globe. Churches of thousands begin with a few dreamers offering new spiritual maps of reality in times of crisis. As one anthropologist put it, modern denominations and churches are simply the relics of previous movements of revitalization. As important as studying relics may be, understanding the powerful forces of change that produced the relics is even more important if we hope to understand megachurches and what makes them tick.

The author points out that one of the key historical dynamics behind movements is that of translation. Pioneered by Andrew Walls, the translation principle has two faces. First is homecoming. Through mission activity, Bible translation, and indigenous witness, a new generation or a new people group sense that God has returned to them. He has come back to them, not in judgment but in acceptance and love. In the homecoming stage the gospel goes deep into the heart of a people's soul and culture. But as the root of homecoming goes deep, the branches of pilgrimage grow wide. The pilgrimage side of the translation principle calls the movement to leave the status quo (often in crisis) and join God on a journey of change and growth. The historical power of this translation principle is immense. Dr. Gitau is one of the first to apply this translation theory to the megachurch phenomena.

Thirdly, this is a story about God. Where is God in the megachurch phenomena in general and the Mavuno story in particular? Dr. Gitau writes as a scholar of megachurches but as an evangelical one. Her God is not a god who sits on high contemplating with various levels of displeasure at the human folly unfolding before him. The author's God is the one we see in Genesis, not just creating the world, but also fighting for his world, creating a movement of faith and change led by Abraham and his descendants "through whom all the nations of the world will be blessed." This is the God who leads his church in all places and ages through Good Fridays of decline into Easter moments of new life and power. Why African renewal and Western decline? Why millennial enthusiasm for the gospel in Africa and millennial indifference in America? There are many reasons, but chief among them is the will of an almighty Father on a mission to make all things new. And his favorite pattern for doing so is the pattern of the cross, where life comes from death.

Read this book if you are interested in megachurches. You will find all the standard stuff about megachurches here. But you will find so much more. The story of Mavuno is a story about fascinating people, swept up in powerful movements, by the Spirit of God on a mission. Who could ask for more? May you be as moved and instructed by this story as I have been.

Acknowledgments

I caught my spark at the fire of several fine scholars of missiology, world Christianity, and religious studies. My first words of gratitude go to Mark Shaw of Africa International University and Center for World Christianity, who patiently mentored me to think as a historian and as a theologian rooted in the local church. The venerable Andrew Walls framed the big questions in our seminar classes and challenged us to tell the new local stories. Robert Priest of Trinity Evangelical Divinity School and Elizabeth Koepping, Afe Adogame, and Brian Stanley at New College, University of Edinburgh, each personalized their contribution in my growth as a scholar. I am also grateful to Caleb Chulsoo Kim, James Nkansah, Henry Mutua, Rosemary Mbogo, and Steve Rasmussen at Africa International University for our interactions. The prodigious writings of Professor Paul Gifford of SOAS (School of African and Oriental Studies) and our vibrant conversations compelled me to think beyond cliché about African Christianity. The story I tell here may be read as a situated response to his keen questions on African Christianity. I must also acknowledge an earlier influence without which this book would not be possible: the foundation I got at University of Nairobi (UON). Now that I am a global researcher, I realize that the broad design of the Bachelor of Education, Linguistics and Literature, program inspired in me the quest to explore large horizons of knowledge, and now I find that even in doing a congregational case study I cannot settle for narrow perspectives.

Thanks to ScholarLeader International, Ignite Excellence Foundation, and Langham Partners for financial support at key points in my scholarship.

Pastors and colleagues at Nairobi Chapel and Mavuno Church—Oscar Muriu, Janet Mutinda, Muriithi Wanjau, Carol Wanjau, Linda Ochola—and the entire Nairobi Chapel family and networks: we share many memories around the stories told here. Professors Marta Bennett of International Leadership University/PCUSA and Diane Stinton of Regent College in Vancouver, you have both watched me "come up" for many years.

Mark Royster, Jim Miller, and Chris Kiesling of Asbury Theological Seminary; Bryan Froehle of St. Thomas University, Miami; and Amos Yong of Fuller Theological Seminary: thank you each for being my cheerleaders as I have worked on the manuscript. Finally, many thanks to my cheerful editor, Jon Boyd at IVP, for many helpful suggestions as we have turned the manuscript into a publication.

Introduction

We zipped past the Nyayo Sports Stadium, under the South C Bridge, past Capital Center Mall, and eased to the right to exit. Sunday morning drives along Mombasa Road were bliss—until you reached Popo Road and joined the long procession heading for the same destination: church. The 9:00 a.m. service was just ending, so the traffic was heavy in both directions. It took us twenty minutes to cover the four-hundred-meter (quarter-mile) stretch off Mombasa Road to the church entrance. At the gate I received a tag from a smiling security guard, drove to the far back, and eased my Nissan Marche into a parking spot.

On this bright September morning, my guest, Yonatan, and I arrived in time to walk around visiting with people before we went to the second service. Yonatan was a student from the University of Geneva doing his PhD research on Christianity in Kenya. On the far side of the church grounds stood small temporary tents flapping in the wind, where a variety of classes that began during the first service were still going on. From a mid-sized tent permanently pinned into concrete on the lower end of the property blasted music at full volume. This was where the teens—or the "Boom Twaff" church—gathered. Nearby, in a row of fenced prefab buildings, parents picked up check-in badges for their children.

We headed to the large tent, an all-weather, permanently affixed, tarpaulin dome designed to seat up to two thousand people. A steady crowd flowed along the walkway lined with blooming dwarf palms. On an elevated patio, about ten ushers, dressed in casual but impeccable black, orange, and white attire, were shaking hands and chatting with incoming congregants. Their clothing was not some coordinated choir garb; they were dressed in their own personal items that reflected individual taste and style. Everyone else was similarly dressed in sharp, casual outfits, though in a variety of colors. Women in high heels did not shy away from showing off a little thigh and décolletage on a sunny day, while polished young men nonchalantly scrolled on smartphones.

I introduced Yonatan to a man who blended in with the meet-and-greet squad. Apparently it didn't completely register who he was until an hour into the service, when the same man walked from the back of the church to the podium up front to preach. "That was the senior pastor we met?" Yonatan asked, an incredulous look on his face. Muriithi Wanjau then duly introduced himself to the crowd of fifteen hundred.

Afterward, as we exited, Yonatan looked around in genuine confusion. "When are you going to take me to the adult service?"

It was my turn to look puzzled. "We've just come out of the adult service," I replied. "And there was one just like it earlier. Welcome to Mavuno Church."

MEET MAVUNO CHURCH

The Mavuno Church began in 2005 when an older church divided into five congregations. In April of that year, the more than three thousand congregants attending the Nairobi Chapel in five weekend services were encouraged to choose a service that would, in a few months, become a new independent congregation. The elders requested that they commit to the congregation that upon relocation would be geographically closest to their residential neighborhood. Nairobi Chapel was going to move to the people. Locations were chosen along the four major roads that connect the city center to the outskirts of greater Nairobi. One chosen location was the southeastern side of Nairobi toward the Jomo Kenyatta International Airport. After a lengthy search for a venue, the team leading the Mombasa Road plant identified South C Sports Club, located on the edge of an older middle-class estate, as the site for their new church plant.

On August 7, 2005, the Mombasa Road Church Plant, renamed Mavuno Church (Mavuno means "Harvest"), held its first service, attended by four hundred adults and children. After the initial excitement, the hard work of settling down began. Every Sunday the team would set up chairs, sound equipment, and decor, and then tear everything down after the church service. Often they would have to clean up the mess left on the premises by night revelers before praying and anointing the grounds to get ready for a worship service. Since the club was a business with a variety of vested interests, Mavuno Church was not granted a stable lease. They occupied the club for over two years on transitory arrangements under which they were constantly susceptible to eviction without notice. Then there was the perpetual challenge of a bad access road that rendered the venue unattractive to would-be church visitors.

The numbers did not grow beyond the original cohort that had been transplanted from Nairobi Chapel in those first two years. The real value of settling in the sports club was the formation of a deeply connected church community with a mission. Congregants were compelled to get to know each other very well, and they got to know their neighborhood and city equally well as they learned to ask the right questions.

Mavuno Church had been commissioned to reach the southeastern side of Nairobi. As a church plant of the Nairobi Chapel, the core members were postcollege young adults. Like its sister church plants dispersed throughout the city during the same season, its mandate from the elders was to reach young adults in the more middle-class parts of the growing city. Initially the task had seemed pretty clear. From the University of Nairobi's vantage point, there was a ready pool of former graduates in the estates whose work, lifestyle, and church preferences would have an educated ethos. Many had often come to Nairobi Chapel through the years. However, the lack of parking facilities had discouraged them from settling in consistently, despite the church's ingenious efforts at coordinating up to seven services on a half-acre piece of land. When the church divided up and moved into the housing neighborhoods, it seemed as though there would be quick numerical growth. But it did not work that way, as Mavuno and other Nairobi Chapel church plants quickly found out. There would have to be significant adjustments to account for the social location or, more aptly, the acute social dislocation of the postcollege demographic.

In June 2008, after two and a half years of intense learning and experimenting, Mavuno Church finally got an opportunity to move out from the shadows of the sports club and into a spacious drive-in cinema off Mombasa Road within reach of several residential estates. Young adults, among whom Mavuno had been creating a buzz and who now found the church physically accessible, began trooping into the all-weather tarpaulin tent. They quickly resonated with the message and invited their friends. Within four months the crowd had grown from four hundred to eighteen hundred. They started a second service, built prefab classes for children, and put up a second tent for teenagers.

By 2012, when I took my friend Yonatan to visit, Mavuno was essentially an impressive, if eclectic, megachurch with close to four thousand adults, youth, and children. The church maxed out the ten acres of the drive-in facilities and began a campaign to purchase and move to its own property. It had also planted a church in Kampala, the capital city of Uganda, and had sent scouting missions across several African capital cities as it prepared to plant more churches. By 2015 Mavuno was meeting in its own permanent location, further down Mombasa Road to the south of Nairobi. The new location was within the reach of a fast-developing residential area around the Athi River. In addition, Mavuno had five additional campuses across Nairobi, five in other African countries, and one in a European country. It also had a transforming impact on the Mariners Church, a large megachurch in Orange County, Southern California. All this happened in under ten years and the momentum is just picking up.

Many people who are familiar with the insider affairs of megachurches around the world will recognize the outline of this storyline: modest beginnings, hidden years of hard work, and then a trigger that sets in motion a season of great numerical growth and publicity. For those unfamiliar with the inner workings, it is easy to take for granted the current success of these megachurches demonstrated by the number of people that attend, the large facilities, and the apparent affluence of members. Social observers of a church like Mavuno that has campuses in the city, church plants in the region, and growing global renown will immediately conjure images of the power and money associated with such franchising congregations.

The term *megachurch* has become the normative reference for churches like Mavuno that attract large numbers of attendees. The numerical marker is placed at two thousand members per weekend service, although many are far larger. Other notable characteristics of megachurches include the demographics of those who attend, including ethnic composition or race, social class, political preferences, age, language, level of education, occupation, appearance and dress, and family relationships. Megachurches may also be identified by the largely middle-class status of attendees (evidenced by large parking lots and auxiliary facilities that are used for more than worship services) and the larger-than-life personalities of their pastors, some of whom make frequent media appearances and exert political influence.[1]

My Argument

I will expand this brief "brochure" version of the Mavuno Church story into a narrative that offers a perspective on the rise, growth, and place of megachurches in the contemporary world. This story will demonstrate that such churches emerge out of the margins, the message initially crystallizing within a demographic that is deeply affected by the crosscurrents of social change. Church communities that grow to a mega size do so because they provide a map of reality for these demographics to navigate a world that is otherwise experienced as deeply volatile.

At Mavuno Church those who constitute this demographic are the millennials, those who were born around 1980 and started to come of age in the new millennium. As they have matured, African millennials have found themselves in transition through several worlds all at once—the vestiges of the traditional world of their grandparents, the modernizing and largely urbanized world of their parents, and the global, technologically advanced world of their own time. Further, in the case of Mavuno Church, this demographic is found in the upwardly mobile and aspirational side of the city. These transitions result in an experience of fluid identity and fragmentation of their life-worlds, which is psychologically, spiritually, and socially destabilizing. Before we can see how these millennials come into their own in the church community, we have to understand how their context of constant transition and fluidity leaves them feeling alienated.

---

[1]Scott Thumma and Dave Travis, *Beyond Megachurch Myths: What We Can Learn from America's Largest Churches* (San Francisco: Jossey-Bass, 2007). As Thumma and Travis use it, the term *megachurch* itself serves the role of a "bounded nomenclature," that is, a distinguishing place marker for a type of congregation, the large one in contrast to the numerous small ones, especially in North America. While their work aims to dispel the negative stereotypes associated with megachurches, in this book I aim to explain why and how they grow and thus their significance in the world today.

For Kenyan and African millennials, the crisis goes back to the modernizing conditions that have shaped the African world over the last two hundred years. These conditions include the colonial experience itself, the accelerated pace of historical change in the fifty years since colonial occupation ended, and the stage of intensified global change stemming from accelerated innovation in information and cultural technology.

The colonial narrative is well-known; what is less appreciated is how the structural incoherence inherited from external incursions has impacted life right up to the present. Without rehashing the ills of colonialism, we can still get to the logic of why, in the pithy Igbo saying, "the rain is beating us" (that is, why "Africa is in trouble"). Prior to the colonial era, most African societies organized social, economic, and political life around kinship and communal needs. Colonial occupation arbitrarily grouped distinct ethnic groups into singular national identities and foreign configurations of political order. The means of production and subsistence were drastically altered, and sociocultural arrangements shaped by both religion and a rational-scientific worldview were introduced.

The postcolonial era not only carried the burden of the new political configurations (nations) but immediately exerted additional pressures, including cold war politics and massive amounts of foreign aid to accelerate economic progress. Among the political arrangements of democracy or socialism, nation-state formation, economic development, and education, Africa has been going through a kind of psychological conflict within itself, rooted in an attempt to cope with the simultaneous political, economic, and social changes introduced from the outside and summed up by the word *modernization.*

In Western societies modernization was a complex process prefixed by a thousand years of preparation and preexisting large-scale organizations (such as the church, the monarchies, and even an elite educated class). Thus, when industrialization and consequent urbanization, expanding scientific knowledge, and faith in progressive human rationality came in full force, it was a natural development at structural, elite, and grassroots levels. By contrast, Africa did not experience the long-term intellectual preparation that took place in Western societies, not because Africans are averse to innovation, but rather because historical contingencies did not allow for this to happen.

Under colonialism and its aftermath, it was always assumed that that adoption of European structures would lead Africa to prosperity similar to that of the West. However, the African world did not go through the comprehensive transformation that took place in the West during the eighteenth and nineteenth centuries. Politically, African nations adopted rational-legal bureaucratic arrangements of democracy and, in a few cases, socialism. Yet because tribal identities are strongly retained, politics fall somewhere between state bureaucracy and contingent patrimonial clientelism. Economically, African nations have had a more ad hoc formation and growth, centering on precarious agricultural commodities and natural resources, especially minerals. Another ad hoc source of economic growth has been infrastructure such as schools, universities, hospitals, and a significant humanitarian service sector. More recently tourism, technology, and real estate have developed, especially in emerging cities.

Thus I suggest that twentieth-century Africa has been going through a continent-wide psychological conflict. In human psychology, cognitive dissonance is the discomfort experienced when simultaneously holding two or more conflicting cognitions, ideas, beliefs, or values.[2] In a state of dissonance, psychologists tell us that disequilibrium is expressed in a variety of ways that render the individual dysfunctional in normal society. We might call Africa's many crises—such as the inability to streamline political power for the common good, the impoverishment of an otherwise resource-rich continent, and the proliferation of violence—reflections of structural worldview dissonance.

Alongside the dissonance, African cultures continue to navigate transitions between the traditional world, the modern urban world, and the globalizing world. The problem is not that Africa is stuck; it is dynamic. The problem is that it has to make sense of all these worldviews in rapidly changing times while making life work for its citizens.[3]

---

[2]The original theory of cognitive dissonance was developed in the 1950s by Leon Festinger. See a recent and more relevant reevaluation of the theory and a variety of applications today: Joel M. Cooper, *Cognitive Dissonance: Fifty Years of a Classic Theory* (Thousand Oaks, CA: Sage Publications, 2007).

[3]For fuller arguments on these issues, see Martin Meredith, *The State of Africa: A History of Fifty Years of Independence* (New York: Free Press, 2006); Patrick Chabal, *Africa Works: Disorder as Political Instrument*, African Issues (Bloomington: Indiana University Press, 1999); Ogbu U. Kalu, *African Christianity: An African Story*, Perspectives on Gender Discourse (Pretoria:

The latest phase of globalization, which has swept not just Africa but the whole world, has further deepened the transitional dissonance. In this new phase, a complex set of related processes has increased connectedness and bred an "intensification of consciousness of the world as a whole."[4] This is evident in three forms: One is economic globalization, seen in arrangements of production, exchange, distribution, and consumption of goods and services across the global highways. The second is political globalization, seen in arrangements for acquisition and application of power and the reactions of those that feel marginalized by the dominant arrangements. The third is cultural globalization, seen in arrangements for the production, exchange, and expression of artifacts and symbols that represent the values, meanings, beliefs, and preferences of the contemporary moment.

I will return to the chokepoints generated by these crossroad experiences in chapter two. For now I simply make the case that all these forces—economic, political, and cultural—have left successive generations of Africans feeling that their maps of reality are not working. The millennial generation in particular has felt the effects of the compounded structural dissonance and has therefore become the most psychologically alienated. Millennials are simultaneously in transitional life stages, acquiring higher education, aspiring and growing toward the middle-class lifestyle, and totally embedded in the modern world through the cosmopolitan city. Among them, the escalation of cultural stress results in a fundamental sense of social homelessness or, in megachurch-speak, "brokenness," usually seen through widespread crime, alcoholism, loosened sexual taboos, antisocial behavior among the youth, structural dissonance in the institutions that serve society such as schools and hospitals, and new kinds of corruption in political processes.

In the face of all this disjunction, numerous voices—from parents and teachers to media pundits, clergy, and politicians—express discontent and uncertainty about the existing order and the troubles of society. Ethnic communities, particularly those that are geographically bounded (rural or

---

University of Pretoria, 2005); Kwame Bediako, *Jesus and the Gospel in Africa: History and Experience* (Maryknoll, NY: Orbis Books, 2004).
[4]Jehu Hanciles, *Beyond Christendom: Globalization, African Migration, and the Transformation of the West* (Maryknoll, NY: Orbis Books, 2009), 15.

national), revert to nativism that accuses perceived outsiders as the cause of their woes. Political processes attempt to address the escalating dislocation through new arrangements of power, but since politics is often entrenched in the old order, rarely do politicians facilitate change rather than preserving the status quo. For those excluded by political structures of power, alternative mobilizing and activism becomes the channel to express discontent, often supported by the deep pockets of those with vested interests.

In such times of social dislocation, religious groups also have their reactions. Fundamental volatility wrought by external forces suggests that the theological and spiritual maps, the ancient paths, have failed. Indeed, it is common in Africa and elsewhere to hear the deprecatory axiom "The church has failed." Thus voices from the theological community prescribe how the church should address the distresses in wider society. Conservatives advise stricter adherence to Scripture, creeds, hymns, rituals, and time-tested traditions. Theological liberals try to restructure Christianity to look more like the dominant culture so that it is more acceptable. Theological radicals under charismatic leaders diagnose the old religious order as part of the problem and seek to return to the New Testament to find a "truer," "fuller," or more "Pentecostal" gospel.[5] The majority of religious folk, lacking trust in existing leadership, simply acquiesce to the flow of the dominant culture; that is, they hold on to religious convictions on a nominal level, so they might poll as Christians, but only pay lip service to a Christian lifestyle. All these groups experience a measure of success, but because they are not able to create a complete map to help society move forward, their differences merely highlight the boundary lines between distinct religious (Christian) subcultures.

These events and processes are going on not only throughout Africa but also, I believe, throughout the rest of the world, including North America and Europe, as seen through recent political watershed events. While I am not saying that megachurches are the answer to these problems, I am arguing that the rise, activity, and success of a church like Mavuno should be seen as a response to the fundamental dissonance of their worlds. These

---

[5]See Richard Lovelace, *Dynamics of Spiritual Life: An Evangelical Theology of Renewal* (Downers Grove, IL: IVP Academic, 1979).

churches work from the ground up with the most alienated demographic to rewrite the map of reality with the gospel as the primary compass. Megachurches in the Global South emerge and thrive because they help this demographic make sense of the world by addressing their social, psychological, and spiritual crossroads.

The early histories of many popular megachurches, such as Saddleback and Willow Creek in the United States and Korea's Yoido Full Gospel Church, bear out this argument. Each came to birth and struggled as a fledgling in times when there were convulsive changes in the wider world, when younger generations were trying to find their place. The leaders in the founding years, usually young men, and those who became core followers initially felt the dislocation as acutely as everyone else in society. Through a series of personal life experiences, a leader and a core group developed sensitivity to the troubled world. Following a turning point, a vision crystallized around a series of apparently ludicrous experiments in which the group attempted the impossible, learning on the go and taking hard knocks, pushback, and even failure before they had visible success and formalized their method. Even then, success is a constant learning curve tempered by ongoing change in the wider world. Still, as their message makes more sense of the world, the revitalized followers ultimately help the rest of the society find its own way forward. This being the case, if more and more Africans are finding their way into or aspiring toward the modernizing world, megachurch Christianity (understood not necessarily in terms of numbers but of practices) will have special relevance in the church's future. This is the story of Mavuno Church. And this in a nutshell is the raison d'etre of this book.

OUTLINE OF THIS BOOK

The first chapter is about Nairobi Chapel, the parent congregation of Mavuno Church, in the 1990s. The key to understanding the leadership of the young pastor, Oscar Muriu, who revived Nairobi Chapel from twenty to three thousand people in a decade is to see his leadership through the lens of liminality, a space in which the old world is decaying and a new world has not yet materialized, but where there are seeds of possibility. In the 1990s national volatility was at its worst. Kenya was distressed under its political leadership, young people were enraptured by newly introduced global-cultural media, and the churches, though active, were strongly subcultural. In his relative lack of ecclesial and political power but proximity to university students, Muriu was uniquely placed to conduct some uncommon leadership experiments. His actions catalyzed the awakening of an educated but isolated generation. One of his key trainees, Muriithi Wanjau, would build on this awakening to mobilize the millennials toward a vision of transforming the continent through the power of the gospel.

Chapter two explores what I call the transitional chokepoints and shows the changes that have affected the translation of Christianity through several generations, eventually rendering Christianity ineffective to address larger social problems. Second, I look at the transition of millennials through globalizing technology and unpredictable local socioeconomic conditions and discuss scenarios of the future. This chapter connects the Nairobi young adult world with the budding "youth bulge" of the continent, full of promise but also possibility of peril. I make the case that the unmitigated transitional influences relativize identity, leading to a sense of alienation in the world. But the bigger predicament lies in a future in which there is either a demographic time bomb or a demographic dividend among millennials. Either way the unintended consequence is the compounding of social homelessness. This is why, at least in the logic of the Mavuno Church leadership team, it is important to reach the millennial demographic with the gospel to inspire and coach it with a value system that will shape a constructive future. This chapter will be of particular interest to those asking questions pertinent to the demographic trends and socioeconomic futures of sub-Saharan Africa.

Chapter three shows how Mavuno Church reaches out to the millennial demographic. While some will quickly connect Mavuno's full-grown method with what is known of Western megachurches, the process of experimentation must not be missed. Muriithi started out with a frustrated effort to teach disinterested millennials how to be Christians. His curriculum and methods eventually matured into a "map" of participation in the dynamic church community. The map is a simple tool patterned after Kenya's sport of long-distance running and thus named the "Mavuno Marathon." The point here is that reaching people who are simultaneously lost in transition and translation is like creating a GPS route—one must assume that they know next to nothing of the gospel and then walk them through each step toward Christlikeness. While the Mavuno Marathon is contextual to Kenyan millennials, the chapter will be insightful for pastors interested in figuring out how to reach new generations anywhere.

Chapter four discusses leadership as it evolved in the dynamic Kenyan and African context. I look at how Muriithi's leadership is rooted in the experience of a Kenyan young man growing up in years of national turmoil and therefore personally affected by the dysfunctional maps. As he matured as a leader, Muriithi turned this crisis into an opportunity to forge new pathways for the next generation. Along the way he was mentored and given opportunities by another equally discerning leader, who helped focus his passion and gifts in a direction where they could make a real difference in the world. He came into his own in the 2000s when he encountered the millennial generation in Mavuno's early quarters in the South C Sports Club. With a team of diversely gifted colleagues, he articulated a message relevant to deep aspirations yet rooted in the transforming power of the gospel. As the message took shape, new challenges emerged and new leadership structures formed in response. Muriithi's training, exposure, and mentoring have led him to understand the continent's dysfunction as a crisis of leadership in a much wider sphere than merely the church. Thus, though still primarily a pastor, he steers his followers toward making desired changes in this wider sphere.

Chapter five shows the impact of Mavuno Church on Kenyan millennials. I frame this impact in terms of evangelical revitalization because Mavuno's activities are identifiable within the tradition of revival movements, where participants are driven by a sense of call to invite the whole world to faith and see the church as the hope of the world. I tell representative stories of members who are transformed at Mavuno and in turn are engaged in transforming aspects of Kenya's public sphere, especially in reclaiming and redefining local cultural identity. I also tell of the far-reaching vision of others whose initiatives are aimed at long-term change. Mavuno's influence goes beyond Kenyan boundaries to an international network of churches that are adopting Mavuno's vision for global mission. Those who are looking for a theological perspective on Mavuno will find chapter five especially insightful.

With awareness that the Mavuno story, like that of many megachurches, is still unfolding, I go out on a limb in the final two chapters. It is necessary to make the connection between a new megachurch movement and two broader realities: the consequences of modernization as an inevitable social dynamic and the place of a Christian movement in the modern world. In chapter six I argue that the rise of increasingly self-conscious and upwardly mobile millennials is tied to the modernization that is now taking root in Africa. Despite lingering problems, there is a wind of change shifting toward a stable and prosperous continent. This brave new world needs a focused theology of how to be "Christianly modern," an ethical vision of the successful aspects of the modernizing processes. But evangelical Christianity, whose pragmatic practices have historically birthed large congregations in growing cities, has in fact already been engaging modernizing processes. The conceptual breakdown lies with our inability to fully apprehend structures of modernization as preexisting social dynamics under which all churches, not merely megachurches, must make sense of reality for their congregants and lead these followers of Jesus along a path that both accepts what is (indigenizing realities) and grows as a countercultural community, as expected in Scripture (pilgrim realities). So chapter six and the conclusion suggest that recognition of modernizing realities is the first step toward valuing the place of megachurches in the contemporary world. Once we understand where they are coming from, we can then revise their less savory practices and encourage their better outcomes.

This is an intense exploration, but for good reason. I write to pull back the curtain on the flattening generalizations in existing scholarship and challenge the common diatribes against churches that emerge out of marginal communities to occupy their own sphere of the mainstream. In the outline of conditions—the background of societal volatility, an alienated generation, leaders whose skills are forged in the chaos, hence whose message makes sense of the chaos of new times, the formation of a following through new leadership structures, and growing influence in the world— some readers may find a frame or a mirror for their own congregations. Yet this is the story of one particular context, a marking of the terrain, not the whole territory, and its telling here leaves out many details. Even the modest proposal in the final chapters merely suggests a direction that further research might go in sorting out and shaping the theologies that emerge out of megachurches and similarly conceived congregations.

MY PLACE IN THE STORY

As with any story told for the first time, the clarity and detail increase with the telling, so let me take a moment to clarify my own relationship to the story. I have direct experience with the sheer grit behind the scenes in congregations that grow from small to mega size. I first joined Nairobi Chapel as a University of Nairobi student around the time when the church was planning to relocate from cramped quarters to a larger property. After receiving my bachelor's degree, I joined Oscar Muriu's internship program to train for crosscultural missions to France or China. But as it turned out, I ended up serving in various capacities at Nairobi Chapel, and later at Mavuno, for a total of nine years, pursuing a graduate degree in missiology in the interim. I served at the heart of the transition from a single congregation to five separate ones. A good deal of this story is therefore told from personal experience of my own and fellow staff members' deeply invested energies, working directly for Pastor Muriu at Nairobi Chapel and later for Pastor Muriithi Wanjau at Mavuno Church.

Even though I have an insider perspective, I do not reproduce the ideas or stories of these communities and leaders verbatim. They do what pastors do best: figure out the life of the church community on a weekly, seasonal, and annual basis. I take the next step of describing in detail and analyzing what I hear them saying and see them doing. I weave the story with an educated perspective on wider social changes, political events, cultural patterns, and even religious developments. As a child brought up in rural Africa and then transplanted to the city through higher education, I not only relate profoundly to the social change but find that much of it was foreshadowed in a wide variety of literature that I encountered while studying for my bachelor's degree in literature and linguistics and later for graduate-level missiology and history. Along with the cast of characters in this story, I was deeply affected by the disruptions of incomprehensible social change. But everything changed when new leaders such as Muriu and Muriithi came onto the scene and, like Moses, led us into a new identity and destiny.

My capacity to tell this story grew even more with the pursuit of a doctorate in world Christianity at Africa International University. I studied under historians Andrew Walls, Mark Shaw, and Brian Stanley, with a one-semester excursion at the University of Edinburgh. I was compelled to face the critical questions raised about Christianity in Africa by the provocative works of Paul Gifford. His prodigious writings on the subject require not just critique but also an articulate response from Africanists. I learned to meet this challenge from the consummate ethnographer Robert Priest, who has devoted himself to training a new generation of African researchers through practical projects such as the Africa Leadership Survey.[6] I also write in light of extensive global encounter through a project facilitated by Asbury Theological Seminary, the Luce-Foundation World Christian Revitalization Study, through which I was able to research in countries with thriving Christian movements in Asia, Latin America, and the United States. Then, to put the whole story together, I scoured a great deal of literature at the Asbury and Fuller Theological Seminary libraries—with Chris Kiesling, Bryan Froehle, and Amos Yong as the captains of my cheering squad during the reclusive study days. Thus shaped by history, missiology, and global encounter, I intend to arrive at an integrated narrative of the dynamic local, regional, global, and theological spheres represented by the rise of movements such as this one. Ultimately, I am convinced that the patterns I find in the Mavuno Church story—of helping new, dislocated generations make sense of changing worlds through the power of the gospel—reflect by degrees the experience of churches that grow from nondescript groups into megachurch movements all over the world. This is megachurch Christianity reconsidered.

---

[6]See Robert J. Priest and Kirimi Barine, *African Christian Leadership: Realities, Opportunities, and Impact* (Maryknoll, NY: Orbis Books, 2017).

1

·····································

Oscar Muriu

Bold Leadership in a Liminal Decade

Nairobi Chapel: Rising out of
a Disoriented Decade

Nairobi Chapel was started in 1952 as a small fellowship for colonial settler families. Since Kenya was a British colony, settlers generally paid homage to the Anglican All Saints Cathedral that met at what was then the edge of Nairobi. But a few families who could not quite fit in with the Anglicans began meeting instead at the Girl Guides headquarters. Their worship services and leadership structure reflected the traditions of the Plymouth Brethren. Congregations in this tradition did not recruit pastors, because they would come from among the elite and congregants deemed themselves sufficiently educated to interpret the Bible without appointed clergy. This group registered as the Nairobi Undenominational Church and built a little chapel near a newly established college that would grow into Kenya's premier research institution, the University of Nairobi. Gaining visibility through a radio program named *The Bible Hour*, they quickly experienced what was then significant growth among settlers and soldiers. However, when Kenya gained independence from the British in 1963, growth was reversed as most of the British returned to Britain. In subsequent years, although the University of Nairobi expanded around the Nairobi Chapel premises, students thought of it as a boring church for old white people and were not interested.

By the late 1980s, membership had dropped to sixteen people, only two of whom were Africans and the rest of diverse European origins. Barely able to keep the lights on, Nairobi Chapel faced closure. The story goes that these remaining members spent six months praying and fasting about the future of the half-acre property on which it stood. They sensed that God was asking them to "indigenize" the church. In 1989 they requested the Reverend Mutava Musyimi, who was then pastor of Nairobi Baptist Church (and would later head the National Council of Churches of Kenya, join politics as a member of Parliament, and subsequently vie for the presidency), to help. Musyimi visited as a pastor for a while and took some time to understand this little congregation. He then explained that to indigenize, the leadership would have to adjust their Plymouth Brethren community to bring on a lead pastor, open up participation in Holy Communion, and create room for young people. Attracting young people would mean rethinking their methods of worship, outreach, and organizing for regular fellowship. Not fully grasping what this meant, the members agreed.

Oscar Muriu, a young man who had a passionate sense of call into pastoral ministry, was at the time just finishing his master of divinity degree at the Nairobi Evangelical Graduate School of Theology. Musyimi had known Muriu for several years, observed his deep commitment to the Lord, and admired his unshakable conviction that he was called to be a pastor. He presented the dilemma of the Nairobi Chapel to Muriu. The only downside, he informed him, was that the little church did not have funds to pay a salary that would be adequate to sustain his young family. Muriu accepted a stipend that was partly subsidized from Nairobi Baptist's funds for a time. Toward the end of 1989, Muriu, his wife, Beatrice Wambui, and a team of other young people from Nairobi Baptist were commissioned to lead Nairobi Chapel.

In a year Muriu was confirmed as the pastor of the little church. With a new focus on evangelism to university students and revamped worship, Nairobi Chapel soon found itself flooded with students who eventually came back as young families. By 1993 the tiny sanctuary that had been built to accommodate under a hundred people was packed with more than two hundred, mostly students. They knocked down side walls to expand the wings, tucked in more benches, and creatively maxed out the space to hold four hundred people. Soon they had to run two services, then three, then four. The numerical growth continued year by year. By the late 1990s,

Nairobi Chapel had to hold seven weekend services to accommodate up to three thousand adults, most of whom were former students now with young families. A separate Thursday night worship service for university students, called SALT (Serving a Living Transformer), was also started. In 2000 Nairobi Chapel embarked on a major capital campaign to move to a large piece of land. However, in another few years the church changed course when it decided to divide up and spread out around the city in five separate congregations. The Mavuno Church was planted out of this decision as a congregation of four hundred members.

What was it about Muriu's leadership that turned this declining church into a successful megachurch and precipitated the success of Mavuno and the other church plants in the next decade?

Muriu was born in 1965 to a father who was a businessman. He attended Lenana High School, a boys' boarding school founded in the missionary era with a reputation as a leading institution for brilliant young men. After high school his father sent him to India to obtain a bachelor's degree in zoology. He came to Christ while he was in India and responded to the call to serve God when he was at a retreat in the mountains of northern India, where he witnessed a Hindu devotee's futile quest to find God by staring into the blazing hot sun. When he returned to Kenya, Muriu was planning to pursue a higher degree in science so that he could serve God as a leading scientist, but Mutava Musyimi challenged him instead to pursue a master of divinity degree to prepare to be a pastor. In 1986 Muriu joined the recently established Nairobi Evangelical Graduate School of Theology (NEGST). This school had been started in 1983 by Association for Theological Education in Africa (ACTEA) as a part of a vision to train evangelical leaders for the growing church in Africa. It was at the end of Muriu's studies at NEGST that Musyimi once again approached him with the proposition that he should pastor Nairobi Chapel.

Muriu was not raised in a church, so even with his theological education, he had to learn pastoral leadership on the job. But this placed him at an advantage, since he didn't have to spend time unlearning old habits and models in order to lead innovatively. Since Nairobi Chapel was also in transition from the old missionary-shaped reality to a new era, there was no preprogrammed script for him to follow as a leader. So he created a path by walking in it.

Initially Musyimi supervised the younger man, but quickly realized that he was wholly capable of thriving on his own. Musyimi stepped back, initially to the loud protestations of the unassuming Muriu. But then Muriu owned his leadership role and gave it his all. When asked how Nairobi Chapel grew phenomenally under his leadership, Muriu would simply comment that the elders who commissioned him figured out, "With a church of under twenty people, we couldn't do much damage. But we didn't know what we were doing. . . . We were learning on the go."[1]

A leadership position is usually understood in one of three ways. Autocratic leadership is based on a traditionally assigned role, usually within an inheritance structure such as a monarchy. Bureaucratic leadership is holding an office under legal or contractual arrangements with stakeholders who have defined responsibilities as well as privileges. Democratically elected leaders, CEOs, and other office-based positions are seen this way. Charismatic leadership is usually contingent to a situation that comes up rather unexpectedly, requiring a gifted personality to rise to the occasion and guide the people. The success of charismatic leadership is based on the intersection of personal gifting and a *kairos* moment. While there are no hard lines between these three leadership models, there are definite expectations associated with each of them.

But this was not the case with the assignment that Muriu came into as a young man; he was simply a pastor. In fact, pastoral work wasn't even referred to as leadership at that time. Muriu was in uncharted territory, particularly because of the marginal place that Nairobi Chapel occupied. Anthropologists use the term *liminal* to describe that place where individuals and society "don't really know what they are doing."[2] Liminality is the threshold between two worlds, one an old, often-decaying order, and a future that is vaguely imagined, yet to take shape. But it is precisely that threshold where there is potential for new possibilities.

---

[1]For this and other folkloric narratives that help to shape this chapter, see "Nairobi Chapel 25th Anniversary," December 18, 2014, www.youtube.com/watch?v=pzM250V8ldM.
[2]Victor W. Turner, *The Ritual Process: Structure and Anti-Structure* (Chicago: Aldine, 1969), 359-73.

The decaying world in which Muriu became the pastor of a nondescript little chapel sandwiched between university residential halls was the 1990s, a disorienting decade for the whole Kenyan population. Under the presidency of Daniel arap Moi, Kenya was experiencing profound confusion. In 1978 Moi had taken over after the death of the first president, Jomo Kenyatta. In the first five years of his rule, Moi fared well under his *fuata nyayo* philosophy—that is, following in the footsteps of the founding president as a unifying leader. Beginning in the 1980s, Kenya, like many African countries, was hit by a series of misfortunes: a failed military coup in 1982, drought and famine, the emerging crisis of HIV/AIDS, and the implosion of the war-torn neighboring countries of Somalia, Uganda, Congo, Sudan, and Ethiopia. Throughout this time Kenya was under immense pressure. Internally, the country fell into disrepair with collapsing infrastructure, endemic poverty, rampant crime, and escalating political dissent. By the late 1980s President Moi's leadership was being challenged by increasing opposition demanding open democratic space through multiparty politics and better distribution of national resources. In reaction, Moi and those closest to him tightened their grip on power in unconventional ways that made Kenyans cower in deference. This was a time of severe political repression, with the disappearance or torture of supposed dissidents. In turn, ethnic communities and the rural poor turned against each other in anarchic conflict.

One of the devastating sects that arose around this time was a quasi-religious group known as the Mungiki. This ethnically fundamentalist group came into the limelight in the early 1990s, following ethnic clashes that targeted Kikuyu people in the Rift Valley Province. Rallying disaffected Kikuyu youth, Mungiki compelled adherents to abandon Western lifestyles and Christianity to worship the traditional Kikuyu god Ngai and to practice ritual customs such as female circumcision and prayer and sacrifices facing Mount Kenya. All this was to awaken the apparently oppressed Kikuyu people. Organizing with army-like discipline, the movement gained a massive following of about two million youth at the height of its visibility. To fund its activities, the Mungiki established a parallel government in crime-ridden, low-income settlements of Nairobi. The movement also took control of the chaotic Matatu transport and construction industries, levying protection tax and dishing out informal justice to offenders in these areas. Basic law enforcement and justice systems were so broken and corrupt that low-income and rural residents welcomed Mungiki protection for a fee. With time, however, these actions spiraled into extortionate vengeance.

While Mungiki had the greatest visibility, there were other similarly organized and politically funded fundamentalist militia groups that galvanized their communities by reasserting traditional lore and identity over against other perceived "enemy" tribes and invasive modernity. Such groups included warriors from the Kalenjin communities, the Sabaot land defense force from the Elgon district, Chinkoro of the Kisii community, the Mombasa Republican Movement from the coastal Kwale district, the Taliban Luo group in Nairobi's informal settlements, and Jeshi la Mzee, among others.[3] Such groups caused considerable civil unrest throughout the 1990s.

FORMING AND LEADING A CREATIVE *COMMUNITAS*

This was the larger world in which Muriu pastored and grew Nairobi Chapel from twenty people to three thousand: one shadowed by poverty, political repression and retaliation, and fundamentalist ethnic mobilizing around traditional lore. Opposition politicians, civil societies, and NGOs all tried to make sense of the chaos through political activism and humanitarian-driven work. A new brand of Pentecostal churches also thrived in this decade (which will be explored further in chapter two). Yet much of this action—whether political, ecclesial, economic, or cultural—only increased the number of dissonant voices without a coherent vision to guide the country to renewal.

Anthropologists point out that the reconstructive possibilities of a liminal period of time lie in both the decaying order and the potential in a forgotten or alienated part of society. Although Muriu jokes that he couldn't do much damage with the few white folks who remained at Nairobi Chapel, they were not the objective of his ministry efforts. The university students were his interest. For all practical purposes the university fraternity

---

[3]P. Kagwanja, "Courting Genocide: Populism, Ethno-nationalism and the Informalisation of Violence in Kenya's 2008 Post-election Crisis," in *Kenya's Uncertain Democracy: The Electoral Crisis of 2008*, ed. Peter Kagwanja and Roger Southall (New York: Routledge, 2013). See also Mahathir, "'Rag-Tug' Militia Groups That Control Kenya," *Muthumbi* (blog), April 23, 2008, http://muthumbi.blogspot.com/2008/04/rag-tug-militia-groups-that-control.html.

was forgotten by the political class. There was plenty of restiveness within public universities, including frequent strikes in protest of botched political processes. But to shush them, President Moi would tell young people to await their turn tomorrow. Likewise, Christians in the university had become disconnected from existing churches. Student movements such as FOCUS (Fellowship of Christian Unions), Navigators, and Campus Crusade (New Life) were quite active in the universities. But these Christian groups were not addressing the volatile concerns of the time and so remained relatively small, as they were deemed out of touch with reality by the majority of students.

Muriu inherited a church that had a successful beginning with the Plymouth Brethren. In its prime back in the 1960s, it had run a radio ministry and attracted quite a following among the British. This history gave Muriu and Nairobi Chapel some legitimacy that was not available to the new, unaffiliated Pentecostal startups that were all over the place. Muriu was not tied down by a board of elders, nor were there administrators to consult on day-to-day decisions. Autonomy from political, economic, and ecclesial control brought opportunities for new and experimental possibilities in evangelism, community formation, and particularly leadership and leadership development.

As a graduate of NEGST, Muriu was aware of how African churches and theologians had wrestled with the problem of foreignness in the structures and methods of the older missionary generation. Throughout the 1960s and 70s, the challenge was to shift power, resources, and structures from the missionary generation to African leaders. By the 1990s, there was not so much a foreignness problem as a generational one. The younger educated generation had increasingly lost touch with the church, and significant portions of the church had become out of touch with what was happening in wider society. Muriu did not come as a prophet to that larger social sphere, but he reawakened the university-educated generation to start to develop a social consciousness that would extrapolate the implications of the gospel for a wider world.

But passing on the agency of the gospel did not necessarily start out as conscious effort. Muriu's passion was simply to evangelize. Recognizing the possibilities that were latent among the intellectually astute students,

Muriu directed evangelism and community organizing activities toward them. He and his team of seven young people from Nairobi Baptist took to the pastoral task of reaching out with the energy of youthfulness. They went door-to-door in the residential halls, witnessing and inviting students to church. For Sunday worship, the trusty old organ was replaced with drums and electric guitars. Hymnals were replaced with the newer technology of an overhead projector. They projected a mix of hymns and contemporary Christian music (at the time the Hosanna! Integrity and Maranatha labels were the trend). A band of young students led music, which stood in contrast both to the more precision-driven music of the missionary hymns and the loud choruses of the Pentecostals. The band not only experimented with musical instruments, but also learned to mix the trendy contemporary worship music with the rhythms of African beats, eventually adding African dress.

Between Sundays Muriu worked tirelessly as he prayed, read, and visited with students. He was convinced that God had a great future for Nairobi Chapel. Praying through Isaiah 54, he asked God to give him thirty students to join him in reaching the university. He followed his prayers with plans to engage first-year students because they would be easier to influence and retain than older students. A buzz spread through the university community, and soon the church was flooded with curious and spiritually hungry students who resonated with Muriu's style of thinking intellectually about the faith. His closeness to them in age was also a huge plus.

A few influences shaped Muriu's intellectual approach. First, trained as a biologist in India, he was adept at using statistical and empirical evidence to prove his point. He would make broad appeal to the scientific and natural world, including his love for gardening. Another influence was his key mentor, the British Anglican pastor John Stott, who occasionally visited and stayed at Muriu's home. A third was his persuasive communication skills, not in the charismatic style of the Pentecostals, but rather honed through disciplined reading of a wide range of literature.

By the mid-1990s, Nairobi Chapel had many former students returning as young families. The Sunday worship service was piped into a room for nursing mothers, which was then a new approach in churches. They put up prefab classroom facilities at the back of the chapel to accommodate the young ones. Muriu's wife, Beatrice Wambui, an art teacher by profession, organized the children's classes according to grades and recruited all her friends as volunteers in children's church. The children's ministry, from the nursery through the teen "Rites of Passage" (ROPES) program, came to greatly appeal to young parents.

Just as with pastoring, Muriu did not have a script for leadership, nor a team of equals to work with. Missionary Omar Djoeandy came on as copastor in the mid-'90s. Djoeandy was a Chinese-Australian trained as a medical missionary in the United States. In answer to God's call, he and his American wife, Kay, came to get a seminary degree at NEGST around the same time that Muriu was also a student. Later they returned and became care pastors at Nairobi Chapel.

The rest of the leadership roles were shaped by the needs that emerged in the growing community in this liminal time. Anthropologists point out that the rise of a new *communitas* is not just about "community" but about the conception of an egalitarian modality of relationships where individuals set aside social roles and status in transitional times. In place of the old structures that assert power, participants in the new community attach to one another as friends who share the same recognizable humanity and relate spontaneously as roles emerge. So at Nairobi Chapel in the 1990s, Muriu was simply "Oscar" to his congregation. He never adopted the title "Reverend" or "Bishop." The rigid boundaries between clergy and congregants, then prevalent in older churches, gave way to collegial relationships as copastors, volunteers, and friends around the roles that were evolving. As Nairobi Chapel became financially successful, Muriu eschewed status symbols such as new cars, fancy dress, and pandering to popular personalities that showed up in his congregation. Only late in the decade did the title "Pastor" become a regular prefix, with the rise of another generation that struggled to differentiate the personal side of pastoral ministry from leadership responsibility and authority.

Muriu devised opportunities and created leadership spaces where his trainees, and eventually colleagues, could find their place to serve. In answer to his prayer that God would give him workers for the harvest field, Muriu began to identify and recruit specific students to mentor. In 1993 he started what came to be known as the Internship Program. Given our familiarity with internships today, it would be easy to undervalue how radical Muriu's idea of developing leaders from within the context of practical ministry was. At the time it was unheard of for a university graduate to spend a year serving in a church, because attaining a university education was such a unique privilege. Also, there was no compensation in an internship. Trainees had to raise support from friends and families, and there was no esteem in clergy work.

For Muriu there was nothing inferior about internship. He created this program as a chance to discover one's calling, to explore and exercise gifts, and to develop new skills alongside others. Interns were given real responsibility and learned how to lead by running the church's ministries under his coaching. They were trained in personal disciplines of prayer, study, and self-care. They would raise resources and spend weeks on short-term mission trips in remote parts of the country or sometimes abroad in other African countries. In subsequent years, interns went on to become pastoral trainees and eventually salaried ministry directors in departments that they created and shaped. They supervised large cohorts of volunteers for worship and creative arts, pastoral care, small groups, social justice, young adults and youth, children, and church planting, all of which grew every year.

Although it was not obvious at the time, this model of the internship inspired an educated demographic to revalue its formal education as a call to be responsible toward the church and wider society. The program raised a generation of leaders who have gone on to assume significant responsibilities in church and social-justice initiatives in which they are also coaching younger leaders. One of the first interns, Janet Mutinda, served as an associate pastor at Nairobi Chapel before moving to become the director of New Life Home. Steve Maina, another of the early interns, led one of the first church plants of Nairobi Chapel, Lifespring Chapel. He later relegated the leadership to another former intern-turned-pastor, Bob Kikuyu, while he went to lead the Anglican Mission organization Church Army in New Zealand. Jane Wathome interned in 1996, then pursued a theological degree at Nairobi International School of Theology. While doing a field practicum, she came face-to-face with the devastating effects of HIV/AIDS, especially on women, in Rongai on the southern outskirts of Nairobi. Jane tightened up her own family spending and asked her friends to do the same, so that they could pool their meager resources to start home-based care for infected and affected women and their children. Her project became known as Beacon of Hope. With the support of Nairobi Chapel members and their networks, including Chapel Hill in North Carolina and Grace Community Church in Indiana, it grew from its early humble stage into a large community center with a hospital and a technical school serving the whole Rongai Township. In just over fifteen years, the center has considerably reversed the devastating impact of HIV/AIDS in the town. Similar projects by former Nairobi Chapel interns include a network of health centers (known as Tumaini clinics) in low-income areas, children's homes, and child sponsorship projects. Numerous others are leading initiatives in the business and corporate worlds.

The internship program also attracted international participants from churches in America, Australia, and Europe, who were fascinated by Muriu's leadership. One couple, Jason and Heather Webb, were sent by Elmbrook Chapel in Wisconsin. After serving for three years at Nairobi Chapel, they returned to the United States and planted Brooklife Church in Mukwonago, Wisconsin. They led the church into significant growth for seven years before being called back to lead Elmbrook. Jason is now the senior pastor of this eight-thousand-member megachurch, which is now planting similar community churches.

SETBACK, RESET, AND A NEW ERA

During the 1990s the number of people worshiping at Nairobi Chapel grew from the original twenty to more than three thousand, and would have grown more if there had been space. Each year the leadership team got more creative in their attempts to accommodate the numbers. At the peak of this innovation there were seven worship services each weekend. On Sunday, there was one at 8:00 a.m., two at 10:00 a.m., and two at 12:00 p.m., the extra two being held in Ufungamano Hall five hundred meters down the road. Two services were offered in the evening: one on Saturday and one on Sunday. Parking on the university curbside was a perpetual headache as the church struggled to create room for increasingly well-to-do congregants.

By 2000 the elders had made the decision to move the church to large premises along Ngong Road on the edge of several middle-class suburbs.

What then seemed like an impossible amount of money to raise, forty million Kenyan shillings (US$400,000), was needed to purchase the land. The church held fundraisers such as women's bake sales and men's golf tournaments. Some involved everybody, such as the walk across the floor of the Rift Valley (famously dubbed the "escarpment crunching walk") and the Mount Kenya climb. The children walked 40 kilometers (25 miles) from Nairobi to Thika; the youth walked 140 kilometers (87 miles) from Thika to the gate of Mount Kenya; the women climbed the first half of mountain; and the men scaled the top of the mountain. Finally the land was purchased, and the big move was planned for 2003.

However, Nairobi Chapel's plans were disrupted by political transition. In December 2002, President Moi, who had ruled the country for twenty-four years, was replaced by the NARC government led by Mwai Kibaki. The winning campaign platform was a promise to fix a wide range of issues from the Moi era, one of which was massive irregularities in land allocation. Early in 2003, the new NARC government froze construction on land near forests. As it turned out, Nairobi Chapel's new land was located on the edge of the Ngong Road Forest. Their relocation was halted.

Stumped, the church leadership entered a new season of prayer and consultation that would last another two years. During this time it became apparent that God was leading them to give up relocating as a single congregation and instead divide up and spread out around the city. To outsiders, as well as some congregants, the move seemed ill-advised because there was so much personal attachment to the pioneering decade of the 1990s. But if hindsight is always 20/20, wisdom is proved right by her children. By the end of August 2005, only one congregation of roughly five hundred people still met at the former Nairobi Chapel site, now renamed Mamlaka Hill Chapel. Everyone else was in one of the four other new plants scattered across the city: Kileleshwa Covenant, Mashariki, Mamlaka, Mavuno, or Nairobi Chapel.

Muriu himself planted one of the congregations near the property originally bought by Nairobi Chapel. Under his leadership Nairobi Chapel continues to focus on raising up the next generation of church leaders. They develop their gifts through a vibrant planting movement, discipleship, and serving the poor through a variety of social-justice projects. Muriu is an internationally well-respected voice in missions who has been invited to speak at many conferences, including Urbana. He is also a frequent speaker in some Western theological institutions.

Yet in retrospect, the real significance of Muriu's influence on Kenyan and African Christianity is that his leadership generated a new indigenous intellectual current that deliberately engages the social implications of the gospel in the local worlds.[4] This first happened at the margins of a university community, but now it is becoming its own kind of mainstream. Though aware of the global influences that are sweeping over local cultures, it seeks homegrown ideas, resources, and solutions that might be available to help new generations determine their destiny. At the same time, it seeks out and is sought for partnerships by churches from around the world. It also shapes church-planting and social ministries that have grown out of Nairobi Chapel and its daughter churches. Nairobi Chapel has had an indirect renewing impact on other churches, which do not always credit it but which demonstrate its influence through leadership development internships, homegrown social-justice initiatives, decentralized multiplication of middle-class churches, and critique of global religious personalities and their media empires.

That said, keen observers of Kenya's recent social, economic, and state bureaucracies note that by focusing his latter energies on outreach to an ever-younger demographic (which his trainees are also doing), Oscar Muriu has himself missed a *kairos* opportunity to help the now-awakened 1990s generation shift to a maturing discernment of the gospel's interaction with national realities. Muriu and leaders of similar middle-class churches that thrived with Kenya's watershed political events—the 2002 and 2008 elections and the 2010 constitutional process—had the social-class base

---

[4]There were earlier cultural-intellectual currents, the most obvious of which was the strong rebuttal of colonialism through African literature. The African cultural theology of the 1960s and '70s was another budding indigenous intellectual wave, but its steam may have been exhausted by the socioeconomic crises of the 1980s and '90s. Within the African cultural theology was the famous debate on missionary moratorium. A related but much less recognized indigenous intellectual current came through the student movements of Scripture Union, Kenya Secondary Christian Fellowship (KSCF), and the college-based Fellowship of Christian Unions (FOCUS), all of which have historical trajectories uniquely shaped by the local and global crosscurrents. The character of these rationalized responses to real-time crises of destabilized worlds has shaped small but important segments of the Christian populations through the decades, but their stories remain to be told in full.

to influence a conversation on the public ethics and moral grounding, now sorely lacking, of the elite that runs corporate and state machinery. In spite of efforts of younger churches like Mavuno to transform the social sphere, the vacuum in ethical leadership among the middle-aged elite is sending the country into a new cycle of dysfunction.

But the energy poured into expansion has borne fruit. Twelve years after relocation, the Association of Nairobi Chapel Churches has become a movement of fifteen thousand people in the church plants and their plants. Today each of these churches is not only an independent congregation loosely associated with the others, but each also has an array of social ministries started and supported by former interns, volunteers, and congregants. Altogether the story of the association is one of grassroots Christianity rising out of the ashes into a dynamic movement transforming the African urban world. Yet despite the success epitomized by the movement's numbers and dynamism, none of the church plants had an easy resettlement in the middle-class residential areas. To demonstrate, this story now turns to Muriithi Wanjau and his team of three other pastors and four hundred congregants who were commissioned to plant the Mombasa Road congregation that became Mavuno Church.

2

Whither African Millennials?

Crossroads and Chokepoints

The Gospel: Lost in Translation

"I give you the right to read and do all that appertains to this degree." This edict was President Moi's popular commission to graduates of the six public universities in the country throughout the 1990s. The charge was somewhat misleading in light of the limited opportunities available to those who graduated from college during his tenure, an era when employment in the public sector all but stagnated. The Nairobi Chapel, nestled within University of Nairobi halls of residence and close to the sanitized precincts of State House, could not paint a clear picture of what became of graduates after their government-loan-subsidized education. Mavuno and the other church plants would soon find out.

South C and its environs—Nairobi West, South B, Makadara, Hazina, Imara Daima, and Langata—were not typical poor, urban neighborhoods; they had been set aside as middle-income housing estates for the civil servants and business class during a sane period of urban planning. Soon two stark realities dawned on the new church planters. First, the suburban neighborhood, here and elsewhere, was populated with churches. In this area the new church planting team was unwelcome because it was perceived as hip and rich and led by a young pastor. Hip and young were perhaps acceptable characteristics for a youth group but not for an actual church.

Second, more ubiquitous than the churches in South C were the pubs and clubbing spots that flanked residential blocks. The patrons of the clubs did not fit the typical description of people that poor urban ministries sought to reach. Rather, this is where the lately minted, newly employed university graduates came for raucous rounds of drinks. Here they would show off their new money, the car just acquired on a company loan, the latest jewelry they bought on a South African holiday. Certainly, employment was hard to come by, but once a graduate secured a job, it was a choice ticket to privilege and pleasure in all the popular joints of Nairobi.

The Mavuno team began to examine this phenomenon more closely and found it to be a consistent pattern in most middle-class housing estates all over Nairobi. There were plenty of churches whose roots were either in missionary-founded denominations, though now independent of missionary leadership, or in the rapidly mushrooming Pentecostal churches. At any rate, all the churches seemed to be in competition with each other. Yet, for the Mavuno team, a stroll through residential parking lots on Sunday mornings revealed that there were many urban dwellers impervious to the electric guitars of the Pentecostals and the bells pealing from towers of older churches.

Recognizing their work was cut out for them, the team experienced a mental shift. They investigated patterns of church attendance in the city. For a starting point, they found research carried out by an evangelistic organization called Finishing the Task in 2004.[1] It showed that at the time only 16 percent of Nairobi residents went to church on any given Sunday, distributed throughout thousands of small church communities across all parts of the city. There were some popular Pentecostal churches based in or around the central business district—such as Maximum Miracle Center, Jesus Is Alive Ministries, the Redeemed Christian Church, Neno Evangelism Center, Winners Chapel, and Nairobi Pentecostal Church—that attracted several thousand attendees each Sunday. (Some have since expanded and moved out of the city center.) There were also many older mainline churches that had a consistent middle-aged crowd. And every so often an international evangelist would draw a huge crowd at the city center's recreational Uhuru Park on a Sunday. Still, in a city of four million people, only 16 percent could be found in church on any given Sunday. Something was not adding up.

---

[1]ACM-FTT Afriserve, *The Unfinished Task: A National Survey of Churches in Kenya* (Nairobi, Kenya: ACM-FTT Afriserve, in partnership with Dawn Ministries, 2004).

To understand the discrepancy, the Mavuno team turned to the non-churchgoing urban crowd, which they found to be a world unto itself, so to speak. This class was employed in government as teachers, doctors and nurses, police, clerks, and so on; in service industries such as banking and tourism; and in the NGO sector that had found a convenient hub in Kenya since the 1980s. As far as church was concerned, the urban crowd had much to say to Muriithi and his team. First, they had a "beef" with the zealous, self-professed Christians, who were perceived as hypocrites who talked about more than demonstrated their love, yet boasted moral superiority. They saw the pastors of the more effervescent churches as overly focused on converts and not interested in real relationships. The whole Christian enterprise was seen as a miserable life of dos and don'ts, prohibitions and control. Christians tended to be judgmental and sheltered from the concerns of those who were different from them. They were also seen to be old-fashioned and out of touch with reality.

Even though Muriithi and his team could see through this caricature, there was a real issue at hand. On the ballot paper and in popular conversation, it was claimed that Kenya's population was 80 percent Christian. Nairobi, with its many missionary agencies, was known as the New Jerusalem of Africa. Kenya had a vibrant Christianity, seen through public visibility of churches and their umbrella organizations such as the National Council of Churches, Evangelical Alliance of Kenya, and the Kenya Conference of Catholic Bishops. There are also many Christian institutions of higher learning, a profusion of parachurch organizations, and numerous NGOs rooted in churches. So it was initially shocking to discover such a low rate of church attendance and so many negative views about Christians. As it turned out, the gospel was lost in translation to this latest generation of young adults.

Muriithi would later frame the problem succinctly in an eight-week sermon series that he titled "This Ain't Your Grandma's Church." He surmised that the problem lay in the degrees of cultural accommodation, co-optation, and reactions within successive generations of Christians since missionary times, through the ensuing decades as Christianity took root alongside the processes of nation-state formation. He described how this happened in three successive age cohorts, leading up to the fourth, present generation, which represents a much younger, self-consciously changing, university demographic.

The first generation consists of those whom Muriithi calls the "converts"— the first to accept the message of the missionaries and the first Christians in their villages. Rejection of Africanness, by embracing Western dress and names, was a precondition for acceptance into the church, ostensibly to acquire a Christian worldview. What was European was Christian, in contrast to the "heathen" ways of fellow Africans. In turn they usually became societal outcasts, ostracized for their faith or relegated to the fringes. Change came to this generation due to the nationalist movements that fought for independence, as well as through the African Indigenous Churches (AICs) that rejected Western ways but redefined Christian teachings in ways that were inclusive of some traditional cultural practices. While they addressed some cultural issues, the AIC churches eventually became segmented into rural and urban marginalized poor. The nationalist movements ditched AIC Christianity as soon as it accomplished its purpose of mobilizing Africans against colonial domination and winning political independence.

Muriithi calls the second generation the "conformers"—the Christians of the period from 1940 to 1960. These would have been educated in the missionary schools at a time when Christianity was increasingly accepted in the culture for instrumental purposes. In addition to sharing the characteristics of the earlier Christian generation, they maintained the same institutions that early missionaries had built with the same leadership structures and social and liturgical arrangements. Recognizing the value of a Western education, they were positioned to take up leadership once the nations were freed from colonialism, but also allowed Christianity to be compartmentalized in the secular-sacred dualism that Westerners themselves displayed. Reaction against this generation of conforming Christians came from revival movements such as the East Africa Revival, which resulted not so much in the breakaway of churches but in the formation of a Christian subculture with a strongly pietistic identity within the existing denominations. As African cities grew, the conforming Christians were absorbed into the changing urban culture with increasing degrees of nominalism and cultural accommodation, while the devout ones strengthened their detached piety.

Muriithi calls the third generation the "adaptors." They were born in the decades spanning the struggle for colonial emancipation, the euphoric independence decade, and the jaded beginnings of postcolonial breakdown (thus Muriithi also calls them the *Uhuru* generation). They went to high schools of missionary origins when the ethos of discipline and religious instruction was still strong. There they learned the rudiments of Christianity, and because they were largely raised in Christian homes by the conformers, they grew up acculturated to Christianity as a way of life. Yet it was not a value system that would inform their daily choices or work ethic. Because it matured without the crisis of colonialism, this is the generation that should have forged a way to integrate Christianity into the building of nationhood, resolving tribal acrimony, addressing the colonial inequitable distribution of resources, creating sustainable wealth, and shaping a social value system. Instead this generation largely gave a nod to Christianity and maintained a religious front whenever expedient, but focused energy on appropriating the elite spaces created in the immediate postcolonial era. They vacillated between Western and African identities, proud to be African but strongly embracing Westernized lifestyles, including their affiliation with a mainstream church and its leadership elite. Reaction against the adaptors came from the classical Pentecostals and later the radical neo-Pentecostal groups who created lively churches that roundly condemned the nominalism of the mainlines.

It is precisely because of the way Christianity took root among these generations that in the 1960s and 1970s a robust theological conversation questioning the relationship between Christianity in Africa and African culture emerged. The underlying presumption was that Christianity was not felt to be relevant to real African problems. Yet if this conversation flourished in the academic circles, its impact in congregations remains open to question.

By the 1990s when the Nairobi Chapel was flourishing within the precincts of the university, much of Kenyan Christianity could be found along two polar opposites. As institutions, mainline churches had carried the ethos of their missionary era into the present. Under the leadership of their umbrella organizations, they were valiantly engaged in a wide variety of relief, development, and social projects, including provision of education, health, and economic development, albeit with donations from denominational counterparts abroad or international donor agencies. In the era of the struggle for multiparty democratic space, key leaders of institutional mainlines joined opposition political leaders to challenge President Moi's government to allow more democratic space; some paid the ultimate price.[2] In terms of spirituality, the actual religious life of the members of mainlines largely reflected the anomie of the wider society in the face of the social convulsions of the day.

Conversely, beginning in the late 1980s through the 1990s, budding neo-Pentecostal churches reenergized the public religious space with new "miracle" churches led by a "big man or a woman of the big God," as Ogbu Kalu puts it in his introduction to African Pentecostalism. These churches were flanked by large open-air crusades, evangelistic bands, and appearances of international evangelists associated with them. They emphasized personal salvation as the cure to social ills. It was a Christianity marked by powerful, evocative preaching. Personal evangelism and conversion was understood in bounded terms and reinforced by clichéd phrases such as "am saved," "praise the Lord," and "Christ is my personal Savior" and plenty of memorized Scripture. The centrality of the Bible was maintained, but it was largely oriented toward boosting personal faith and success. To this group of Christians, on any issue Jesus was "the answer," a claim followed by proof-texting Bible verses. Muriithi observes that this Christianity did not learn to ask, "What is the right question?" It rather held the naive assumption that if everyone got "born again," all problems in society would be solved. This Christianity was reinforced by a subculture of its own parachurch organizations, televangelist celebrities, and books brought in from Western evangelists. The 1990s saw the emergence of strong apocalyptic themes, which seemed to be validated by world disasters and reinforced by wild apocalypse-themed books that were flooding in from America

---

[2]Paul Gifford, *Christianity, Politics, and Public Life in Kenya* (New York: Columbia University Press, 2009), 36-37; NCCK Secretariat, *A Century of Ecumenism and Mission: The Story of National Council of Churches of Kenya, 1913-2013* (Nairobi: National Council of Churches of Kenya, 2013).

and Nigeria. While these themes subtly shifted again toward personal success and achievement in the millennium decade, many Pentecostals remain enthralled by apocalyptic eschatology.

All these generations of Christians filled important gaps in otherwise difficult decades, without which the country and the whole continent would be far worse off. Missionary-founded mainline churches have stood at the heart of the history of the country and continent as providers of education and social services. In response to perceived nominalism, reactive religious movements were also attempting to rewrite the map of social and religious realities in the face of confusing change. As for the followers of various Christianities, these were their attempts, in the apparent power of the Holy Spirit, to make sense of life in the almost-surreal destabilization of their worlds.

In the logic of Ogbu Kalu, each older church or Christian movement has paved the way for newer and hopefully fuller expressions of the gospel.[3] For instance, although the missionaries isolated early converts from their communities, these isolated converts translated the Bible and became readers and teachers to the next generation. The creative syncretism of sectarian and often irrational AICs revalued the traditional African worldviews in their own Christian way. The challenge that the AICs posed to the more mainstream Christianities compelled the mainstreams, especially their theologians in the 1960s and '70s, to confront the foreignness of their own churches and to call for indigenization, inculturation, and contextualization. It also birthed the more pious revivalist spiritualities, such as the East African Revival, the classical Pentecostals, and the high school and university student movements, which also had their day. These brands of revivalism often thrived at a time when the nations were economically, politically, or otherwise incapacitated. Whether by fluke or by proxy, each generation of Christians has had a renewing influence on the next generation. Kenyan and African society would be socially worse off without the churches, so historical retrospection must lend grace to each generation for doing what it could.

That said, the churches' shortcomings are valid to the point at hand. Emmanuel Katongole starts his book with that rather incongruous

---

[3]See Ogbu Kalu, *African Pentecostalism: An Introduction* (Oxford: Oxford University Press, 2008).

observation that "churches and coffins are perhaps the two most prevalent images associated with Africa today."[4] If churches and coffins represent the two predominant cultural realities, they also represent the predicament of a continent suspended between hope and pain, beauty and tragedy, dreams and frustrations. Africa is at once overwhelmingly Christian and at the same time politically, economically, and socially distressed. Jesse Mugambi, writing in the 1990s Kenyan context on liberation and reconstruction, similarly decried this contradiction.[5] Paul Gifford, following nearly two decades of research on Kenyan Christianity, also arrives at the contradiction of a highly vibrant and visible Christianity on the one hand, and a nation in which political impunity is the order of the day on the other.[6]

These observations made at the academic level describe the gulf that Muriithi and his team found in the middle-class residential neighborhoods between a Christianity that was irrelevant to current social and cultural questions and a young adult demographic that didn't even care. By the time Mavuno was planted in 2005, the next generation was largely lost to these older Christianities at a fundamental level. The legacies of the past had bequeathed a faith that was felt to be out of touch with reality. In the late 1990s and into the new millennium, an influx of programming from America had brought in Christian television and music that generally propagated a Christianity that, in the words of Muriithi, "is both dangerously naïve and mind-numbing towards local issues." Consequently, Christianity has formed language and mannerisms that are only intelligible within itself. The other spheres of society gave a nod to Christian rhetoric but considered it irrelevant to real problems except in times of crises, such as those generated by politics or disease.

Once they realized that the gospel had never been translated in terms intelligible to this generation, the Mavuno team knew that they could never be reached using the traditional methods of evangelism or even by appeal to the church as a self-evident social reality or cultural prerequisite. Reaching the millennials would require a complete rethinking of the message, the

---

[4]Emmanuel Katongole, *The Sacrifice of Africa: A Political Theology for Africa* (Grand Rapids: Eerdmans, 2011).

[5]Jesse Ndwiga Kanyua Mugambi, *Christian Theology and Social Reconstruction* (Nairobi: Acton Publishers, 2003).

[6]Gifford, *Christianity, Politics, and Public Life.*

medium of communication, and the methods of building community. In a country so presumably Christian, that was a tall order. Hence the Mavuno team had to consciously disengage from the traditional identity of a "church," even the identity they had brought from Nairobi Chapel in its predictable university environment. The team first worked to forge an identity as a countercultural community. To do this, they began to study the lifestyle, work habits, entertainment, communication, relationships, and other life patterns of the postcollege Nairobians.

The team then crafted a profile of the sort of person that would not be found either in the older mainline churches or in the Pentecostal churches but would rather party on weekends and sleep in on Sunday mornings. They created profiles for these types of people and named them "Mike" and "Makena," a man and a woman, both in their twenties, aspiring to a cosmopolitan lifestyle, with corresponding consumption and relational habits. These profiles would be adjusted over the years to reflect the changing realities of the Mavuno congregation. At the time, the trial and error sketches became markers to determine how to plan worship, preaching, and community activities for the club-hopping crowd. Other elements, such as strategy, vision, and sense of mission, took protracted conversation within the team. They eventually hammered out a neat mission statement: "Turning ordinary people into fearless influencers of society." A strategy plan known as the "Mavuno Marathon" became essential to fulfilling this mission. Mavuno's vision to "plant a culture-defining church in every capital city of Africa and gateway cities of the world" would take shape much later when the church began to grow numerically.

THE SOCIOCULTURAL ARENA: LOST IN TRANSITION

Before I discuss Mavuno's message in detail (see chapter three), let me pull the curtain back on the solidarity that Mavuno Church developed with the postcollege millennials. This happened first in the microcosm of South C, but its logic was later extended to the city and other capital cities in the continent. This section builds on chapter one's narrative of the events of the 1990s to show the simultaneous crossroads experiences and cultural chokepoints that postcollege urbanites faced. This will clarify why Mavuno Church designed its message, medium, and leadership as it did.

Muriithi chose to identify the young adult postcollege group in Kenya as the "8-4-4 generation." This designation refers to the 8-4-4 system of education, which was definitive for those in this age bracket. This in turn has implications for how we view their attributes, needs, and contribution to local Kenyan society. Since this system of education is still in use, in some ways the same characteristics continue to apply to the emergent young adults in the early decades of the new millennium.

An inefficient education system. Kenya's immediate post-independence system of education was structured as 7-4-2-3 consisting of primary, secondary, and tertiary or university education. As the immediate heir to colonial education, this system was designed to prepare an elite workforce to serve a population then largely perceived to be illiterate and unskilled. The intention was for graduates to take on white-collar jobs left by settlers and missionaries, such as doctors, teachers, and civil servants in the new economy. The nation would, in the logic of modernization, develop in similar ways to Western nations. But by the early 1980s, it was clear that modernization was not happening along Western parameters and the system of training elites was not equipping new student cohorts to solve the real problems of the developmentally challenged economy. In 1985 Kenya tried to redress this by introducing a new system of education known as the 8-4-4, that is, eight years of primary school, four in secondary, and four in university. The intention was to diversify the formal academic curriculum with vocational and technical education at each level of schooling to impart practical skills and attitudes of self-reliance. When one left the 8-4-4 school system, one was expected to either find gainful employment or alternative ways of being self-employed.

However, the changes in curriculum structure did not constitute a real change in the mentality of educators or in the resources that the government allocated to educational institutions. A popular *benga* song of the 1980s and '90s carried the mood: *Someni vijana, muongeze juu ya bidii, mwisho was kusoma, mtapata kazi nzuri sana* (Read, young people, put more effort in your studies. At the end of your school cycle, you will find very good jobs). But that is not how it worked. The economic and political conditions in the country were not conducive to creating new jobs in mainstream professions of education, government, security, and medical fields. As opportunities diminished, nepotism became the way to secure the little formal employment available.

While it provided basic and even intermediate literacy, that system of public education continued to churn out graduates who accumulated educational credits but not problem-solving skills. In response, a resourceful private sector of education, consisting of both secondary and tertiary institutions (and, significantly, rooted in the church) emerged to redress this weakness, largely supplying graduates to work for the active NGO sector in the entire region. Still, this only catered to the minority of the urban population that could afford private education. To add insult to injury, the ill-advised structural adjustment programs (SAPs) of the 1980s had caused loss of civil service jobs so that the parents of the 8-4-4s were themselves struggling. The local community and national political conditions, the absence of free press, poor mediums of communication, and a centrally controlled banking industry did not encourage individual enterprise. To show such initiative was to invite the ire of small and big power brokers in the clientelist political system of the time. So the first problem that 8-4-4 generation faced as it came of age was the absence of real employment and other economic opportunity.

Influx of external cultural cargo through liberalized airwaves. In the 1990s, a new, initially devastating, influence swept across urban centers in Kenya, further alienating already jaded young adults. This was the influx of global media through the liberalization of the Kenyan airwaves and media industry. Up to this point, Kenyan airwaves had been monopolized by the Kenya Broadcasting Corporation (KBC), the single national broadcaster of both television and radio, which also acted as the mouthpiece of the single-party ruling government. In 1989 the Kenya Television Network (KTN) was introduced as the first private television station. Although associated with the ruling class, KTN was seen as a welcome recourse from the monotony of "patriotic" programming aired by KBC media. Soon other private media houses were licensed, including NTV, Channel O, East African TV, and Citizen TV. Capital FM radio was introduced in 1996 as the first private radio station.[7] These were the harbingers of what is now a

---

[7]Paul Musau, "The Liberalization of the Mass Media in Africa and Its Impact on Indigenous Languages: The Case of Kiswahili," *AAP* 60 (1999): 137-46.

flourishing media industry that has more than one hundred radio stations and more than twenty television stations throughout the nation.

According to local elite observers, what immediately marked the new media was the liberal nature of its programming. With its quest for quick profits and popularity, the emerging free enterprise brought in foreign content indiscriminately. The influx of "cargo," such as the Spice Girls, the funeral of Princess Diana, Whitney Houston's fame and infamy, and pop sensation Michael Jackson, along with stale soap operas from Mexico and the emerging American hip-hop phenomenon, into urban Kenyan living rooms all at once "clogged the airwaves with dirty, out of date, content."[8] While the benefits of technology were potentially enormous, and did in fact become critical to the economic turnaround in the millennium decade, the theories of globalization that link mass media to cultural imperialism (Americanization) are well demonstrated in what happened in Kenya in the 1990s: broadcast media alienated people from the local customs and cultures that had shaped previous generations. Hegemonic cultural influence then led to a loosening of previously held certainties and attachments that formed social bonds. Everything coming from the outside appeared to be superior and more desirable, especially to the young people. This relativized local values, cultural traditions, and representative social imaginaries.

In a particularly cynical world like Kenya in the 1990s, the globalizing cargo swiftly polarized society as urban youth dumped what respect they had for customs and traditions for the apparently more glamorous, imported content. On a previously unseen scale, youth adopted hip-hop music and its mannerisms, along with American pop-cultural idols, particularly the African American hit-music wonders, whose mutinous lyrics, gangsterism, and hedonism best articulated defiance toward the old order.[9] Even the names that emerging local artists used to popularize their music, such as K-rupt (corrupt), Necessary Noize (noise), Nameless, Kleptomanics, and Nonini, reflected this rebellion against the existing order. Much of it was a harmless release of bottled-up frustrations, but some of it led to a spike

---

[8]Bantu Mwaura, "Kenyan Youth and Entropic Destruction of a Hopeful Social Order," in *Cultural Production and Social Change in Kenya: Building Bridges*, ed. Kimani Njogu and Garnette Oluoch-Olunya (Nairobi: African Books Collective, 2007), 67-69.

[9]Faith Nguru, *Foreign TV Shows and Kenyan Youth* (Nairobi: Nairobi Academic Press, 2013), 177-84.

in crime and fed the unlawful activities of fundamentalist movements such as Mungiki (discussed in chapter one), while some, as we will see shortly, desacralized religious sensibilities. The alien cultural diet was not only psychologically alienating but also paved the way for a consumerist and hedonistic culture on a new scale. The "youthful exuberance"[10] in fact masked the apparent hopelessness of a nation which, caught in deeper political and economic crises, was desperately trying to escape but lacked leaders to show it how.[11]

Desacralization of cultural and religious sensibilities. With the liberalized airwaves, Kenya's 8-4-4 generation was the first to grow up with widespread access to foreign media. As the 1990s came to a close, this generation was also the first to be immersed in the latest revolution in information technology. In the decade of the millennium they would become fully engaged in the social-media worlds of Facebook, Twitter, Instagram, WhatsApp, Snapchat, and LinkedIn as part of their daily script. But by the time the information technology made its full entry into the nation, the millennials had already made a cultural turn that influenced politics, social life, and religion.

The turn began just before the new millennium. The most vocal and culturally accepted group that triggered this awakening was a comedy troupe known as Redykyulass. While the turmoil of nationhood would need full political processes to turn the corner, Redykyulass catalyzed a transition toward a new era of global connectivity.

Kenya, as noted, was a country under immense pressure in the 1990s. President Moi, the quintessential "big man" of Africa was a force to reckon with.[12] As the country was pressed by a series of misfortunes and caved into the disrepair of collapsing infrastructure, endemic poverty, and rampant crime, Moi tightened his grip on power in unconventional ways. The late 1980s and early 1990s were times of severe repression, with the torture and public derision of supposed dissidents; the decade of political

---

[10]Mwaura, "Kenyan Youth," 71.

[11]The sort of social change described in this chapter is illustrated by comedian and *Daily Show* host Trevor Noah in his revealing, recently published memoir about his South African childhood and teenage years: Trevor Noah, *Born a Crime: Stories from a South African Childhood* (New York: Spiegel & Grau, 2016).

[12]Alec Russel, *Big Men, Little People: The Leaders Who Defined Africa* (New York: NYU Press, 1999).

activism barely dented Moi's power.[13] Considering the denominational divisions among clergy and Moi's own claim to devoutness, isolated statements from dissenting clergy such as Henry Okullu, Timothy Njoya, Ndingi M'wana a' Nzeki, David Gitari, and Alexander Muge had little effect. Even after the liberalization of the airwaves, Moi remained popular in Kenya. He was an odd sort of father figure, because alongside his apparent spirituality, he and his elderly, male-dominated political clique systematically hegemonized old-age veneration. His ubiquitous presence through public infrastructure and photographs in civic offices was matched only by his beguiling piety. These two otherwise valuable mechanisms of maintaining social order—religious piety and age—became embedded in the dysfunctional political system, to the extent that even during the worst national crises, the political elite always managed to look clean and untouchable. Most of Kenyan society remained cowed and indifferent to this spellbinding control.

While opposition politicians, with their various political parties, aligned and realigned in an attempt to unseat Moi, it was the youths that created the comedy troupe Redykyulass who most radically challenged the age-dominated political clique. The publicly visible faces of this troupe were three students of Kenyatta University: Tony Njuguna, John Kiarie, and Walter Mongare. Their stage name, Redykyulass, is a parody of the word *ridiculous,* because their comedy capitalized on giving people a good laugh by ridiculing the ordinary and commonplace, slowly disarming preposterous behaviors and expectations. After some theatrical performances at a university cultural week, they became popular in Nairobi and secured space on television. What makes the trio significant to this narrative was how they challenged the hitherto revered leadership vested in age, as typified in President Moi and his closest allies. Moi habitually dismissed the youth as "leaders of tomorrow," an avowal that effectively stifled any contributions

---

[13]Public figures who challenged that power, such as Bishop Alexander Muge and politician Robert Ouko, met unexplained demises. Others such as Kenneth Matiba, Timothy Njoya, and the late Wangari Maathai experienced public humiliation or incarceration in the infamous Nyayo house chambers, where they were broken through torture. See Godfrey Muriuki, "Kenya's Historical Experience: An Overview," in *East Africa in Transition: Communities, Cultures, and Change,* ed. Joseph L. Brockington and Judith Bahemuka (Nairobi: Acton Publishers, 2004), 144. See also Gifford, *Christianity, Politics and Public Life,* 36-38.

they might make to the current debate on national problems. What the youth heard was "Shut up and fall in line."

Redykyulass overturned that condescension. With carefully constructed comedy they satirized absurdities of the sociopolitical scene. They humanized Moi's friends as men who have all kinds of ordinary experiences like eating, dancing, sleeping, arguing, visiting the toilet, and so on.[14] Watching their videos on YouTube today, their act looks so passé compared to their comic successors, such as Churchill and Eric Omondi, whose airbrushed and rehearsed melodrama offers a little more than a socialites' hub. At the time, Redykyulass's groundbreaking parody fractured the cowered silence in Kenyan public culture and initiated critical engagement among the public, clerical, and political classes. This pursuit of alternative ways of engaging with political issues also assisted the politicians' efforts to rally together to end the era of Moi through a national coalition of opposition parties. The self-reflexive laughter held up a mirror to Kenyan society to show how it had been complicit in keeping dysfunctional political cultures alive.

The turn to social reflexivity also enabled a related turn: the millennials' break with the older generation and all that was hitherto venerated. Previously the youth were mostly circumspect in their rebellion. With the help of Redykyulass, the youth learned they could doubt Moi and his men; they also became comfortable with casting doubt on elders, teachers, pastors, and basically all social order. In confluence with the culturally alienating diet of the liberalized airwaves, comedy—especially the type found on early-morning radio, egged on by the consumerist impulse for quick profit in the media industry—caricatured everyone and vulgarized the most serious societal issues. The pendulum of cathartic laughter and demythologization of power swung too far toward the desacralization not only of authority but also of the sensibilities that informed religious values in the psyche of the nation.

For the churches, deconstruction of political and social hierarchies extended to vulgarization of the previously revered sensibilities of the

---

[14]Grace A. Musila, "The 'Redykyulass' Generation's Intellectual Interventions in Kenyan Public Life," *Young* 18, no. 3 (August 1, 2010): 279-99; see also Njogu and Oluoch-Olunya, *Cultural Production and Social Change.*

gospel, namely prayer, Scripture, the authority of clergy, and even moral consensus about right and wrong. Youth came to see these as having been used to legitimize impunity; if one could question President Moi (even stone his car on the day of transition from his rule), everything else could be deconstructed. To be sure, the entire society did not develop consensus on these responses, nor was God banished out of the public sphere to a private religious consciousness. But Christianity became domesticated through a rhetoric that saturated the public sphere but was robbed of its power to witness or motivate personal change.[15] Thus by the time Mavuno Church was planted in 2005, the young people in the South C nightclubs could cynically caricature Christians as clueless and out of touch with reality.

The bigger picture of alienation among global millennials. Several decades back, Peter Berger wrote about similar transitions in the Western world, at the time from a highly religious society that was moving into what he saw as a newly irreligious world.[16] Berger noted that the prior influence of Christianity in the wider society depended on self-evident, social arrangements of faith, which he referred to as *plausibility structures.* Modernization progressively undermined these previously taken-for-granted structures, so that they lost their intactness or continuity, leading to what Berger saw as the secularization of society.[17]

A similar break took place in Kenya in the late 1990s and early 2000s. With all these layers of compounded volatility, influx of new media, and a comedy troupe articulating the deepest grievances in the preposterous candor of comedy, sensibilities that were once intrinsic carriers of transcendent meaning to life started to be seen as vulgar, instrumental, or simply regarded with indifference. To be sure, secularization in Berger's

---

[15]This is part of the central thesis of Gifford, *Christianity, Politics and Public Life.*

[16]Peter L. Berger, *The Sacred Canopy: Elements of a Sociological Theory of Religion* (New York: Anchor, 1969).

[17]Berger describes secularization as the process by which sectors of society and culture are divested of religious power. Ecclesiastical authority is removed from the system of education and politics, replaced by science as an autonomous, secular perspective of the world. Patterns of religious consciousness change subtly in the wider society, so that the effect on the totality of ideation and cultural life is observed over the course of time, not in the short run. Berger, *Sacred Canopy,* 107-9; see also Bryan R. Wilson, *Religion in Sociological Perspective* (New York: Oxford University Press, 1982), 101.

sense is observed strongest within societies that have had opportunity to evolve through a much longer historical process. At this point in the African situation, we are not dealing with secularization in the same sense. What took place was a process of desacralization as the radical youth parodied absurdities of power, entitlement, and impunity vested in the older (political) generation. Hence, old age and figures of authority were divested of their sacralizing value on a scale that had not been done before, shocking the older generation that the young had gone so far. When traditional underpinnings of right and wrong begin to look old-fashioned in the face of modernizing media and the eyes of intellectual-cultural trendsetters, morality takes the first hit as young people throw off what they see as the shackles of tradition. That's exactly what happened, as a new wave of moral laxity threatened to tear the fabric of society—for instance, through the crisis of HIV/AIDS, which President Moi declared to be a national disaster in November 1999.

It is now possible to come to terms with why, despite its preexisting vibrancy and all its contributions through the decades, Christianity did not have transforming relevance to social, political, and cultural issues. First, the process of diffusion through the decades (converts, conformers, and adaptors) was also accompanied by degrees of cultural accommodation in political and social worlds. Second, by the turn of the millennium, Christianity was lost in translation to the 8-4-4 generation, the demographic most affected by the global cultural baggage and newly emboldened to speak out against tradition. Muriithi would therefore say that whereas earlier generations absorbed the contradictions, the gospel would not make sense to the 8-4-4 generation in its old forms, because unlike its predecessors, this generation is cool with questioning and doubting everything. The traditional forms—bound to the sacredness of church, to the respect of parents, pastors, teachers, and others that would corroborate traditional values, methods, and symbols—are largely seen as part of a vulgar world. Although the Pentecostal street preacher still sets up his soapbox, he is regarded a quaint curiosity. The church building is one more ordinary storefront in a cluster. And even in school, the teacher is seen to be a talking head, a means toward a paper diploma, not a real source of knowledge. It is not that the gospel itself has lost its transforming power and meaning, but what once functioned as intrinsic carriers of transcendent meaning to life are now instrumental, vulgar, or simply subject to indifference.

The compounding effect of the technological turn. When I talk about compounded dissonance, I mean that there were many issues pressing at the heart of the Kenyan people. Redykyulass was only responsible for the self-expressiveness and the public language part of the desacralization and domestication. The other reason is that while the vacuum of the first half of the 1990s was filled by imported broadcast media, by the end of that decade the youth had quickly developed self-expression through technology. Mobile phones were introduced in Kenya in 1993 but remained unavailable to the public until the end of the decade. In 1999 the Communications Commission of Kenya was established, and soon after, Safaricom (which would grow into a giant telecommunications company) was licensed to provide mobile phone services. Other communication companies such as Airtel would follow. With cheap tariffs, mobile phones acquired immediate popularity. Internet was introduced in Kenya in 1995, and inexpensive internet access cybercafes in most urban centers quickly popularized all the products of the internet. Open market–based competition on voice and data tariffs has enabled the mobile phone and internet industries to thrive exponentially in a symbiotic relationship. They now offer interactive and differentiated means of connectivity, choices, and tastes that are central to the construction of millennial individual and social identities, including their values. These identities are also intertwined with structural processes of national and global consciousness, affecting business and cultural exchange in crucial ways. For instance, in 2007 Kenya launched Mpesa, a financial services platform that completely transformed economic transactions, created thousands of small businesses for low-income earners, and facilitated growth in many other industries, even the banking sector that initially rebuffed the innovation. Mpesa is now a world-famous mobile money service offering deposits and transfers, local and international remittances, withdrawals, bill paying, and even savings schemes that completely bypass the credit card. The cumulative result of all these developments is that, as of 2017, over 70 percent of Kenyans use the internet, mostly on mobile phones.

For Muriithi, then, reaching the 8-4-4 generation with the gospel means first of all acknowledging it cannot be heard in the old, tried, "sacred" forms anymore. But that does not mean the youth have turned their back on the gospel. The gospel just needs to come to them through the medium that has become their heart language due to daily use—that is, social media.

The riddle of the "great leap forward." At least for Muriithi, the opportunities created by technological developments also raise the ante of why it is important to reach the millennial generation with the gospel at this point in history. This has to do with the polarities of the narrative of a rising Africa.

When information technology became a new catalyst for worldwide connectivity in the 1990s, one phrase that came into regular usage was "global village," referring to the shrinking of time, space, and distance through all kinds of technology. The laptop, the mobile phone, and the internet are the technical tools for this expanded global consciousness and global reciprocity. They have quickly made inroads across Africa, just as they have in all other parts of the globe. Whereas earlier eras depended on slow, diffusive social change, the increased density in communication and the expanded village have restructured and reconnected community, particularly among the 80-plus percent of the young people who are literate across the African continent. Looking at this transformation, global economists have grown accustomed to referring to Africa's shift from primordial communication to the information era as Africa's "great leap forward." This is the view that because of access and use of technology, Africa is poised to take a leap into rapid economic growth, to catch up with the more developed world. The narrative of Africa rising has been prominent in popular media.

There is some credence to this view. As in the case of Kenya, the widespread use of technology has resulted in empowerment of individual initiative, creating substantial improvement for individuals, small and medium enterprises, even some measure of the national economy. Kenya is further ahead than it would have been without the information connectivity. Yet this account only tells half the story; technology comes with its own Promethean penalties, not least the constant relativization of local cultures and local products by ever glossier global ones.

There are also the ghosts from the past. Africa inherited structures designed for Western sensibilities, which in turn foster the principles of capitalist economic development, jurisprudence for maintenance of social order and responsible civic (political) engagement, medicine to deal with disease, and science and technology designed elsewhere. These, at least in theory, are what have put the Western world at an advantage, so the rest of the world aspires toward them. The problem is not these structures *per se*, but that the prospects are tied to fledgling and often fragile states, where the conditions of nation building—state bureaucracy, law, national economies, urbanization, and formal education—have not overwritten cultural and ethnic differentiations that existed before the colonial nations. Earlier I talked about this resulting in a worldview dissonance. The nations are struggling to come to terms with the discrepancies while embracing the ideals of democracy, free market economies, and global technology. Yet the insecurities of state bureaucracies tend to promote ethnic patronage, a ghost that Africanist political scientists would like to be rid of but the evidence, even from stable (Western) democracies, points to the contrary. The socioeconomic institutions that were built in the early postcolonial years are unequipped to cope with the changes of the twenty-first-century world, resulting in performance impasses between older technocrats and younger, technologically savvy ones. "It's Our Turn to Eat," Michela Wrong's damning account of blatant corruption in Kenya in the 2000s, is a mantra for every new ethnic community that gets political representation in the highest office.[18] This is not even to mention the stiff competition for diminishing resources across the globe, where Africa is constantly shafted.

Across Africa, as elsewhere in the globe, communities are reverting to organizing around ethnic identities: loyalties driven by Mungiki-like fundamentalist ideology, where religious, ethnic, or nationalist feeling is at the root of ongoing civil wars and arbitrary violence. Displaced youth become easy recruits into radical activities such as terrorism, insurgency, urban gangs, or more recently, social-media mischief, creating a whole new era of disintegration. Though we would like to circumvent the dilemma, it is impossible to elude the fact that the issue is rooted in the absence of

---

[18]Michela Wrong, *It's Our Turn to Eat: The Story of a Kenyan Whistle-Blower* (New York: Harper-Collins, 2010).

homogenizing worldviews from the beginnings of these nations—a problem, in Katangole's terms, with the "founding narratives" of the continent.[19] The 2004 environmental Nobel Peace Prize Laureate Wangari Maathai explains the restlessness as a long shadow from the past.[20] Much critique of contemporary events in Africa assumes that these ghosts have been exorcised, but as Katongole, Maathai, Jesse Mugambi, and others see it, all postcolonial generations continue to struggle with the disruptions and effects of these invasive influences, while trying to raise the next generations and deal with external centrifugal forces of change.

THE WRITING ON THE WALL: AFRICA'S YOUTH BULGE

This historical dysfunction is having the greatest impact on the 8-4-4 generation, which as it comes of age constitutes the largest percentage of the population in Africa and will continue to be on the rise for the next several decades. That the African population is rising at a phenomenal rate and will continue to do so is the real question.

Compared with the geographic size of other continents, Africa has no lack of space to hold a large population. A map of the "true size" of Africa (see figure 2.1) generated by computer graphics artist Kai Krause corrects world cartography that presumes on the space and capacity of the mother continent.[21] While not entirely to scale, this map shows that the African landmass can accommodate those of China, the United States, India, and Europe with room to spare.

---

[19]Katongole, *Sacrifice of Africa*.

[20]Using the example of her Kikuyu community, Wangari notes how the disruptions from the colonial era cast a long shadow on postindependent Kenyan and African communities. Due to their proximity to "white highlands" that were annexed by settlers, the Kikuyu tribe was adversely affected by colonial expansion. Arrangements of colonial economy, the world wars, and the Mau Mau struggle separated large numbers of Kikuyu men from their families. A whole generation was traumatized by these encounters, leading to the erosion of traditional cultural stability. On the other hand, the proximity meant that the Kikuyu were also the most integrated into the colonial economy. Upon independence, Kikuyu elite reaped the most benefits of the new order, but systematically isolated their poorer kin. By degrees other Kenya communities also experienced similar disruptions of their functional traditional ways of life. Wangari Maathai, *The Challenge for Africa* (New York: Pantheon Books, 2009), 22-23; see also David Anderson, *Histories of the Hanged: Britain's Dirty War in Kenya and the End of Empire* (New York: Norton, 2011); C. Cagnolo, *The Akikuyu: Their Customs, Traditions, and Folklore* (1933; repr., Wisdom Graphics Place, 2006).

[21]David McCandless, "The True Size of Africa," *Information Is Beautiful* (blog), October 14, 2010, https://informationisbeautiful.net/2010/the-true-size-of-africa.

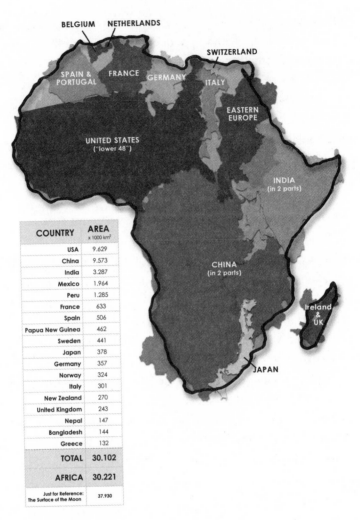

COUNTRY	AREA x 1000 km²
USA	9.629
China	9.573
India	3.287
Mexico	1.964
Peru	1.285
France	633
Spain	506
Papua New Guinea	462
Sweden	441
Japan	378
Germany	357
Norway	324
Italy	301
New Zealand	270
United Kingdom	243
Nepal	147
Bangladesh	144
Greece	132
TOTAL	30.102
AFRICA	30.221
Just for Reference: The Surface of the Moon	37.930

Figure 2.1. The true size of Africa

This vast geographic territory, which has been called the potential bread-basket of the world, could provisionally hold the populations of all these other continents. It currently houses 1.2 billion people, out of a world population of 7.3 billion.[22] United Nations data records that the median age

---

[22]United Nations, "World Population Prospects: Key Findings," working paper, Department of Economic and Social Affairs, Population Division, ESA/P/WP 241 2015. As of 2015, 60% of the global population lives in Asia (4.4 billion), 16% in Africa (1.2 billion), 10% in Europe (738 million), 9% in Latin America and the Caribbean (634 million), and the remaining 5% in North America (358 million) and Oceania (39 million).

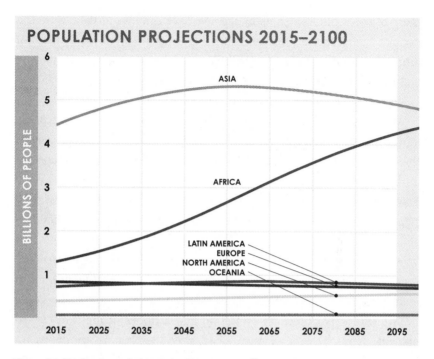

Figure 2.2. Regional population projections, 2015–2100[23]

of the world is 29.6 years. About one quarter (26 percent) of the world's people are under 5 years of age and 62 percent are 15-29 years old. Comparatively, the median age in Africa is 19.9 years. As of 2015, children under 15 account for 41 percent of Africa's population, and young persons aged 15-24 account for a further 19 percent, meaning that 68 percent is under the age of 24.[24]

According to a 2015 UN report, Africa has the highest rate of population growth: 2.55 percent annually. Demographers predict continuous exponential population growth from the current African young-adult population. Barring catastrophe, a large number of young people will reach adulthood in the coming years and in turn will have children of their own, so that an additional 1.3 billion people are projected to be born in Africa by 2050. As

---

[23]Adapted from United Nations, "World Population Prospects."
[24]United Nations, "World Population Prospects"; see also Katindi Sivi, *Youth Fact Book: Infinite Possibility or Definite Disaster?* (Nairobi: Institute of Economic Affairs and Friedrich-Ebert-Stiftung, 2010); and Katindi Sivi et al., eds., *Youth Research Compendium* (Nairobi: Institute of Economic Affairs, 2011).

more of these children come of age and have children of their own, this population is expected to continue rising substantially through the year 2100, meaning that the region will play a central role in shaping the size and distribution of the world's population for at least a century.

That astounding fact is cause to pause and think.

At this point, with 68 percent of the population under the age of 24, Africa is just a young continent with a youth bulge. A youth bulge is when the largest share of a country's population is between ages 15 and 29, during a stage in the nation's development where infant mortality is reduced but mothers still have a high fertility rate. The result is that for a significant period, a large share of the population is composed of children and young adults.

A population bulge requires different types of resources at different age stages.[25] Young children and their mothers need health facilities. On reaching school age, children require educational resources. Older youth need institutions of tertiary education and facilities of life-skills development, then jobs with adequate salaries. As they mature and settle, infrastructure for housing and mobility is needed. If these resources are available, they become economically productive to the country. If working-age individuals can be fully employed in productive activities, other things being equal, then the level of average per capita income in a nation should increase, and the youth bulge will become a demographic dividend, meaning an increase in the productive population—a middle class. However, if a large cohort of young people cannot get good education or find employment to earn a satisfactory income, the youth bulge will become a demographic bomb which implies any number of potential crisis situations in a nation.[26]

---

[25]One vivid metaphor for a population bulge is that of a large animal swallowed by a snake. The bulge can be seen passing through the long body of the snake as it digests over a long time. The huge bulge is present at one point, but with time it passes and spreads out through different parts of the snake. Africa's youth bulge is like the large lump along the head or neck of the snake right after it has swallowed. See Graham Fuller, "The Youth Crisis in Middle Eastern Society" (Institute for Social Policy and Understanding, 2004).

[26]Justin Yifu Lin, "Youth Bulge: A Demographic Dividend or a Demographic Bomb in Developing Countries?," Let's Talk Development (blog), January 5, 2012, http://blogs.worldbank .org/developmenttalk/youth-bulge-a-demographic-dividend-or-a-demographic-bomb-in -developing-countries.

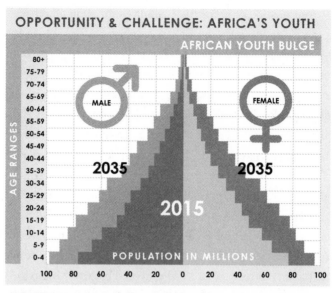

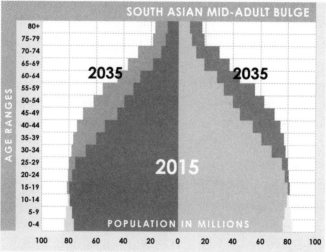

Figure 2.3. African youth bulge vs. South Asian mid-adult bulge[27]

So, despite the conscious awakening of a generation, the economic growth enabled by technology, and the rising levels of education across the continent, the real question at hand is what kind of social, political, and

---

[27]Adapted from "World Population Prospects: The 2010 Revision" (report, 2011), www.un.org /en/development/desa/population/publications/pdf/trends/WPP2010/WPP2010_Volume-I _Comprehensive-Tables.pdf.

economic future is foreseen for the current youth bulge in Africa? Herein lies both the potential and the peril: Will the youth bulge turn into a demographic dividend or time bomb? There are two scenarios, both linked to economic and political developments: the negative one to a dysfunctional continent, the positive one to a prosperous, middle-class continent.

Demographic bomb: Volatile nations. A demographic bomb portends a crisis in a nation or continent. We may be familiar with the extremes of conflict in countries like Central Africa Republic or South Sudan, but it is insightful to see how such scenarios unfold. Kenya first faced this kind of negative situation in the early months of 2008 when the country's exceptional status as a stable nation nearly came crashing down like a house of cards. In 2002 the country had ushered in the new millennium on a high note of optimism after a coalition of opposition parties unseated President Moi and formed a government of national unity led by Mwai Kibaki. Although there were significant gains, Kibaki's side of the government reneged on the political agreements that had led to the victory. In 2005 the fractured government collapsed acrimoniously. Politicians fueled ethnic polarization, while corruption in state bureaucracy reached a high watermark. These issues were exploited in heated political rhetoric throughout 2007, leading to a poisoned election at the end of 2007. After a standoff in vote counting, the incumbent president, Mwai Kibaki, was controversially declared winner in the late hours of December 31. Aggrieved opposition leaders contested. Lacking trust in the judiciary, their supporters took to the streets throughout major cities and towns in Kenya. Between protests and retaliations, the explosive result was nearly a month of burning, looting, and lawlessness that rendered business, communication, and transport impossible. At least a thousand people died, as hundreds of thousands were displaced into squalid camps. Kenya came to the brink of a civil war before a panel headed by former United Nations Secretary General Kofi Annan mediated an uneasy peace and brokered a deal for a coalition government formed of the two conflicting sides.

When the fires of violence exploded, evangelical churches in Nairobi rallied their congregants and collected seventy tons of supplies worth millions of Kenyan shillings (tens of thousands of US dollars). They formed a caravan of two hundred pastors with five buses and drove across the

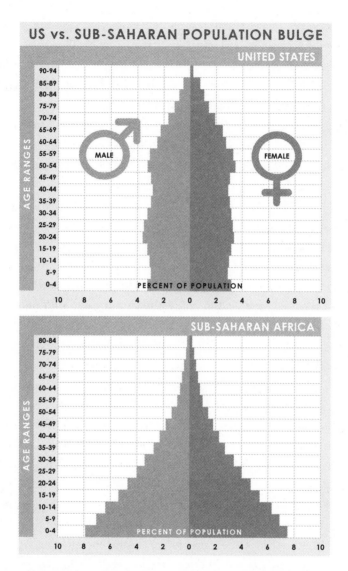

Figure 2.4. US population bulge vs. sub-Saharan African population bulge[28]

country, bringing relief supplies, reconciliation meetings, and cleansing prayers into hot spots of violence. Muriithi was one of the main leaders of this caravan. Previously sheltered in middle-class Nairobi, he came

---

[28]Adapted from "Interop Technologies Analyst Articles," July 6, 2015, www.interoptechnologies
.com/en/analyst-corner.php?year=2015&article=africa-is-poised-to-leapfrog-its-way-to
-wifi-calling.

face-to-face with the heart and heat of the postelection violence. All across
the nation the caravan looked into the angry faces of disillusioned, trapped,
and helpless young people. These youths had lost all hope for any meaningful future as offered to them by politicians' partisan rhetoric. Driven to
the brink of despair by an inept political, judicial, and economic system,
youth had nothing to lose if they burnt the entire system down and along
with that destined the nation to chaos and oblivion. Unless a different
vision of life was offered to them. As he tells the story, this was a defining
moment in Muriithi's leadership career. He returned to work a changed,
charged man. Mavuno's mission of "turning ordinary people into fearless
influencers of society" took on a new urgency. He had to lead the church
to offer lasting and realistic hope to the African continent or die trying.

   Demographic dividend: A middle class. The opposite potential of a
changing continent is the demographic dividend. This is when a high
portion of a nation's population enters the working age with potential to
be productive and contribute to the growth of the economy. It is argued
that with rational, consistent, and effective policies modeled on capitalism,
Africa should forge vibrant economies that will catapult it into an era of
prosperity. The political will is there. A recent report also showed a steady
economic growth over the past two decades, accompanied by the emergence
of a sizable middle class that approximates three hundred million Africans.[29]
For instance, in 2010 Kenya ushered in a new constitutional dispensation
amid great optimism over the future. A development blueprint called
"Vision 2030" had been launched just two years earlier, which intended
to make Kenya a middle-income nation by the year 2030. As a result of
such efforts in many of Africa's stable countries, there continues to be
optimism about Africa's economic future.[30] One encouraging sign is the
World Bank estimation that the number of people living in poverty on
the continent has declined. If the youth population transitions safely into
a demographic dividend, then we will end up with a rising middle class.

---

[29]African Development Bank, "The Middle of the Pyramid: Dynamics of the Middle Class in
Africa," *Market Brief,* April 20, 2011, www.afdb.org/fileadmin/uploads/afdb
/Documents/Publications/The%20Middle%20of%20the%20Pyramid_The%20Middle%20of%20
the%20Pyramid.pdf.
[30]World Bank, *Africa's Pulse: An Analysis of Issues Shaping Africa's Economic Future* 5 (April 2012).

In terms of the economic prospects of the continent, this is good. During the transition from feudal societies to industrialized capitalist societies in the West, the term *middle class* served to describe an intermediary social stratum, a class of society that was neither rich nor poor. In the nineteenth and twentieth centuries, the emergence of a middle class in the West was closely related to the growth of the so-called white-collar workers, who formed a significant part of the urban, social infrastructure. Graduating from universities in large numbers, they became lawyers, doctors, lecturers, managers, and administrative experts in the growing economies of the postwar West. Taking a definite shape during a period of reconstruction of war-torn Western society, this middle class valued and emphasized education, hard work, and thrift, and thus gave impetus for new ideas of capital accumulation.[31] Throughout the twentieth century, this class morphed into the largest group of wage earners, as civil servants, self-employed craftsmen, professionals, and entrepreneurs. In other words, the emergence of this Western class was closely linked to the changes in the social structures that also stabilized Western societies, nurtured capitalism, grew cities, and later gave rise to service industries, including technological ones. The point is that the middle class was both the result and the driver of the brave new world of modernization, concomitantly the mainstay of political regulation, economic liberties, and social stability.

In contrast, the markers of the recent global middle class, including Africa's, have shifted.

While Western nations have had two hundred years to shape their middle class, the formation of the new class is occurring over a compressed time period across the developing world—and the urban middle class feels the pressure in acute ways. There are no longer guaranteed jobs in the older industries and professions that nurtured that earlier class. The increasing number of those who are highly educated is also accompanied by rising population and diminishing resources, so the competition is much greater. Once they find jobs, today's middle-class citizens have to work harder in impersonal, competitive systems to keep succeeding.

---

[31]Clara Brandi and Max Buge, "A Cartography of the New Middle Classes in Developing and Emerging Countries," Deutsches Institut Für Entwicklungspolitik, Discussion Paper 35 (2014).

Consequently, the emphasis has shifted from production and democratic stabilization toward consumption power, loosely defined as households with daily expenditures between US$10 and US$100 per person in purchasing power parity. Given this wide margin, the middle class is now a socioeconomic group whose habits as national and global citizens are highly heterogeneous, depending on the part of the globe they are in. The contemporary middle class is defined by the growing number of households that have access to disposable income that enables them to direct their money toward discretionary purchases such as homes, cars, electronic appliances, and better educational opportunities. They acquire lifestyle debt to maintain conspicuous consumption and competition with socially significant others. What this means is that the so-called middle class is an aspirational class rather than an actual class. It is a lifestyle that engenders strong psychological and social tensions, which are then numbed with a hedonistic lifestyle. This leads to a variety of dysfunctions within families, including high rates of divorce and poorly parented children. Not surprisingly, this class can barely pay attention to values that build up democracy, good societal morals, or investment in the future generation. Instead, to live up to the expectations and the lifestyle that today's middle-class status engenders, it is driven by its pursuit of enablers of a material culture.[32]

Much of the economic transformation that is creating this aspirational middle class is also occurring in the midst of troubled political realities inherited from the past. Observers pinned their hopes on the burgeoning class to be enablers of reform, social progress, and democratization. Ipso facto, the logic of contemporary democratic competition, controlled by minority elites who manipulate the majority poor through mass media, leads the middle class to believe they are no longer vested in solving the wider societal issues, so long as their own bounded sphere is not threatened. As public intellectuals such as Wandia Njoya observe of the emerging Kenyan middle class, for instance, these citizens live in gated communities with private security, so they are not too worried about the growing slums; they can afford private insurance, so if the public health sector fails, they

---

[32]Leslie L. Marsh and Hongmei Li, *The Middle Class in Emerging Societies: Consumers, Lifestyles and Markets* (New York: Routledge, 2015), 2.

will not lobby the government; and their own class runs private schools, so they will not fight for improved national education.[33] In other words, the sense of national identity and democratic ideals is not strengthened by the middle class. The only real benefit that the middle class gives back to the nation is the tax money that is painfully extracted from them. On the other hand, those that do not manage to enter this privileged status watch enviously from the sidelines of grinding poverty. These polarities are the cause of ethnic fundamentalisms and radical extremisms among the marginalized all over the world, not just in Africa.

UNINTENDED CONSEQUENCES: SOCIAL HOMELESSNESS

Amidst the ever-present social flux of the nations, the intensification and compression of the global and local change, and the uncertainties of the future lies the creature predicament: social homelessness. Either way, demographic dividend or demographic bomb, the outcome is social homelessness.

In the late 1960s, when the Western world was coming to terms with the legacy of modernization, sociologist Peter Berger used the phrase *social homelessness* to describe the changes he saw. Modernization, rooted in powerful new economies, technology, growth of cities, structures of state bureaucracy, multiplicity of scientific theories, and increase in media voices, produced a new world. With the progress came cynicism about entrenched social problems such as racial divisions, poverty, and the specter of nuclear annihilation in the wake of the arms race of the Cold War era.

Berger observed that the effect of these macrosocial changes on the individual was enormous. Modernity created "discontents," who were feeling "out of sync" in the universe. Modern discontents, as Berger saw them, were peculiarly "incomplete."[34] They entered adult life with a lingering feeling that "something is missing." In traditional societies, one's place was easily fixed through the life stages of primary socialization. Modern education created new stages of life called "youth" and "young adulthood," which were previously unrecognized. This open-ended,

---

[33]Njoya Wandia, "#LipaKamaTender Is No Longer a Strike; It's a Movement," *Love and Revolution* (blog), January 27, 2017, www.wandianjoya.com/1/post/2017/01/lipakamatender-is-no -longer-a-strike-its-a-movement.html.

[34]Peter L. Berger, Brigitte Berger, and Hansfried Kellner, *The Homeless Mind: Modernization and Consciousness* (New York: Vintage Books, 1974), 77-78.

"incomplete" quality engendered psychological strains that make the individual peculiarly vulnerable to shifting definitions of identity and therefore easily impressionable, especially to the capitalist juggernauts of marketing and image consciousness.

Related to this aspect of being "incomplete," the young adult is unstable. The premodern world was much more coherent, firm, and possibly inevitable as the socialization processes fixed life roles early. The modern individual is bombarded by plural sources of information, which provide multiple options to construct life. The plurality of social worlds relativizes every one of those life-worlds, and therefore the structures of each world, including family, church, community, or even the political order, are experienced as unreliable. To compensate, the individual seeks a foothold in the self and the senses, focusing on feelings and experiences, while the boundaries of self frequently shift to accommodate changing influences from multiple worldviews.

Third, the modern individual is markedly philosophical. In the past the basic presuppositions of one's social world were taken for granted and were likely to remain with the individual for life. One was at peace with one's lot; therefore, one entered a predictable pattern of life early. The modern kaleidoscope of social experiences and meanings compel the individual to make daily decisions, creating tension and rationalization about anything that impinges on identity. The self frequently becomes an object of anguished scrutiny.

Fourth, the modern person is peculiarly individuated. In the past, one was concerned about fitting into group norms. But modern individual rights are taken for granted as a moral imperative of fundamental importance. This is legitimated by the variety of choices in ideologies, mass media, and the shopping mall. As a result, it is easy to cast blame when the world goes wrong, especially on those who represent the old order—parents, government, school, and church.

Berger concludes that the open, differentiated, reflective, and individuated person is afflicted with a *state of being an alien* in his or her own world. This is the condition he calls social homelessness. Forty years after Berger's observations, contemporary sociologists such as Robert Wuthnow, Jeffrey

Arnett, Donas Freitas, and Christian Smith have observed similar characteristics of the present-day young adult in the Western world.[35]

I think the situation of the millennial young adult is no different around
the rest of the world, even in Africa. The dramatic growth of higher education across the globe first expands this global consciousness of the modern
dislocated self. The postcollege adult enters the world of work as an "in
between" person, no longer a child but not quite an adult. The fluidity in
the job market means that stable, lifelong careers have progressively been
replaced with lower security positions and thus more frequent job changes
and ongoing re-education to adjust to the changing needs, including those
changes driven by government agencies. Further, unstable job markets
push emerging adults toward exploring life's options, including extended
schooling, delayed marriage and child bearing (while pursuing sexual
options), travel, and transient living, with a bias toward maximizing personal happiness. These decisions are highly influenced by the networks of
the new social worlds—mass and social media, mobile connectivity, and
school or career contacts.

As Berger saw it, and later sociologists have confirmed, the fixed
boundaries and stable structures of society that once lent overarching
meaning to life have been dissolved by the current conditions of life.
The fractures and loss of loyalty to the institutional fabrics mean that
family, school, church, and stable government cease to be homes to the
self. The individual at once distrusts the outside world and at the same
time turns to the "subjectivities of the self" in the quest for meaning
and fulfillment. Finding no answers inward, modern men and women
become frustrated, emotionally deprived, and constrained—or, in
megachurch-speak, broken or prodigals in their worlds.

Berger's expressions of social homelessness—peculiarly unstable, incomplete, anguished, and open—describe the life of the postcollege urban

---

[35]Robert Wuthnow, *After the Baby Boomers: How Twenty- and Thirty-Somethings Are Shaping the Future of American Religion* (Princeton: Princeton University Press, 2007), 11; Donna Freitas, *Sex and the Soul: Juggling Sexuality, Spirituality, Romance, and Religion on America's College Campuses* (New York: Oxford University Press, 2008); Jeffrey Jensen Arnett, *Emerging Adult-hood: The Winding Road from the Late Teens Through the Twenties* (New York: Oxford University Press, 2004); Christian Smith et al., *Lost in Transition: The Dark Side of Emerging Adulthood* (New York: Oxford University Press, 2011).

millennial that the Mavuno Church planting team came face-to-face with in the clubs of South C. At the time Berger was analyzing this situation, change in the Western world was vividly painted as the countercultural outburst called the cultural revolution. Today, the non-Western world, particularly Africa, is in a similar stage of self-consciousness. This social self-consciousness is not new on the continent (a powerful literary renaissance swept through the continent in the 1970s, and the African cultural theology was part of that movement), but this consciousness is sharpened by a convergence of realities that produce alienation from older institutions, distrust of the present, and uncertainty about the future. Today's alienation may not be expressed in widespread counterculture, as conditions are not favorable. Nevertheless, there are a variety of short-lived social revolutions in different places, such as Mungiki-like fundamentalism, the excesses of liberalized airwaves, and a parenting generational gap.

However, I do not write about social homelessness to fuel the narrative of Afropessimism. Rather, the analysis throughout this chapter helps to show how amid the cultural conflict of compounded worldview dissonance, generational transitional struggles in the face of new globalizing forces, and the prospects of the future, Mavuno, under the leadership of Muriithi Wanjau, recognized what its mission had to be: to reach the millennial generation "ordinary people" and turn them into "fearless influencers of society," who will transform country and continent. In chapter five, I will show how some of these transformed millennials are also transforming their city and in effect resolving these cultural conflicts.

This discussion also shows why Mavuno Church makes such a comprehensive attempt to engage millennials in its mission, vision, and accompanying practical activities. To some measure, churches of all backgrounds hold a similar concern for the continent and the younger generation. Most churches can see the brokenness in communities; many decry the worldliness behind it. Some will say that the problem is with the structures of society, such as government, and will charge politicians to do better. Many churches will call the young people to return to a closer following of Scripture. Many will turn to cathartic spiritual experience through worship, prayer, and other charismatic experiences that bring personal healing. Some will pursue regeneration through small community. All these are valid and have their place, but they often proceed with a partial understanding of the extent of the problem, thus their actions make only a small contribution to the solution. In the next chapter, we'll see how Mavuno Church has stepped out with a much more comprehensive plan of transformation, the Mavuno Marathon.

3

....

Comprehensive Missional Transformation

The Mavuno Marathon

Mizizi: Retracing the Basics

Kenya is globally famed for its long-distance, marathon-winning runners. Long-distance running is a grueling sport that requires extensive training, great endurance, and paced progress. Though it is a competitive individual sport, champions say that winning is easier if they pace as a team. Several times in the New Testament the apostle Paul uses the metaphor of running to refer to the lifelong experience of faith and service. In Acts 20:24, he cites the race as a task he has been given by the Lord Jesus to testify to the good news of God's grace. In 1 Corinthians 9:24-25, he talks about the self-discipline it takes to grow into Christlikeness, where core characteristics of the Christian life are cultivated in a long pilgrimage.

Mavuno Church's core process of "turning ordinary people into fearless influencers of society" is modeled on the time-honored sport and powerful biblical metaphor of a race. This comprehensive mission and discipleship process and leadership strategy is called the Mavuno Marathon.

Muriithi and his team did not design the Mavuno Marathon out of the theological or sociological analysis that I explored in the previous chapter. The Marathon started out as a down-to-earth class teaching a bunch of millennials how to be Christians. As a younger pastor at Nairobi Chapel, Muriithi oversaw a discipleship class for new believers. The course material was borrowed from an interdenominational parachurch organization, originally designed for an American audience. Although the content looked good, those who came to class responded in two different ways. One group, mostly those raised in rural areas, would enthusiastically engage in prescribed spiritual activity such as prayer meetings, crusades, and church attendance. They read their Bibles and prayed, spent time with other Christians, listened to the "right" music, and focused on making it to heaven. On the other hand, some new Christians, mostly urban, postcollege young adults, were quickly bored with this type of Christianity. After the initial excitement of "accepting Jesus," their enthusiasm would flag and they would soon "backslide" into old lifestyles. This group could not connect with the clichéd Christianity. They wanted to follow Jesus but also be real in their social worlds, have unbelieving friends, and be unapologetically successful.

Muriithi recognized this as a pattern in broader Kenyan Christianity. For the enthusiastic "saved and safe" Christians, faith was mostly about personal blessing and security after death. The script of evangelism had little to say about how the Christian life mattered in this world. The work of "ministry" was left to clergy, and faith did not influence decisions about family, parenting, work, or current political challenges. For Muriithi, this explained why a nation could poll as 80 percent Christian and 34 percent born again with so little impact on the world.

Once he awoke to this reality, Muriithi set aside all the discipleship material and approaches imported into Kenyan churches. He recruited an eclectic group of thirty millennials and offered to teach them how to be Christians. To divest of the culture of "freebie discipleship" in which Christians had become accustomed to getting free books and Bibles shipped from outside, he set a "price" for his class. Participants would have to "count the cost" (Lk 14:28-32) to remain in his class. Financially, participants would pay for study material, food, and outdoor events. Timewise, he required a daily investment of thirty to forty-five minutes to read, pray, and prepare for group discussions, along with the two hours of class every week. Another time investment was in group activities, spread over four Saturdays during the ten-week class, including prayer, street evangelism, social-justice visits, and a final weekend retreat. Relationally, he would have no pious spiritualizing during class discussions. He would be totally honest about his real-life issues, needs, and points of growth; in return he expected total honesty, acceptance of responsibility, and empathy for one another from his students. He challenged participants to tell the good, the bad, and the ugly of their actual life histories. This was a radical ask at this point in time, but to his surprise the experimental class accepted his "terms and conditions" and they got the ball rolling. These financial, time, and relational commitments would become part of Mavuno's DNA.

With the Bible, some resource books, and the fresh questions that participants brought to class in hand, Muriithi would write new material each week. The materials consisted of a daily reading, an application point, weekly Scriptures to memorize, and group activities to anticipate. Group meetings would discuss these lessons in connection to real life. Over the weekend, the class would take on practical activities. One Saturday was set aside for scripted prayer and fasting in a retreat center, another to share faith in the streets, another to visit a needy community, such as a prison or children's home—places where sheltered class participants would previously not have ventured. Accordingly, class conversations became animated and forward looking. In the final retreat, participants told dramatic stories of life change. An adventure was born.

At South C, the Mavuno team polished the experimental experiences into a foundational course, published the manual, and called the class Mizizi, "Rooted."[1] As the leadership began to understand the millennials better, they designed and streamlined other activities around Mizizi. For example, the question of how to bring indifferent millennials to a Mizizi class led them to go where those people were—the nightclubs. When a very large cohort took a Mizizi class, they had to find a big enough challenge for the social-justice weekend. They took the class to spend time with prisoners, which is how the annual "Spread the Love" prison outreach was born (more on this in chapter five). When classes completed Mizizi, they wanted to stay together, so they formed "life groups," that is, groups for life, resulting in more than 70 percent of the congregation being in small groups. Muriithi's copastors looked into additional teachings that would strengthen the lessons in Mizizi class, which resulted in a definitive sermon series as well as classes such as Hatua, Simama, and Ombi (discussed in the next section, "Steps of the Mavuno Marathon"). Mizizi unlocked the mystery of how to lead millennials from a place of complete

---

[1]Muriithi Wanjau, *Mizizi: Growing Deeper in Your Faith* (Nairobi: Clear Vision Media, 2005).

indifference to the gospel toward a life of full discipleship. This is how the Mavuno Marathon evolved and became the way to "turn ordinary people into fearless influencers of society."

STEPS OF THE MAVUNO MARATHON

Core to the design of the Mavuno Marathon is the idea that conversion and discipleship are not separate processes but closely linked. They are not a sprint but rather a lifelong journey that involves encounter, learning, and growing in a course that resembles the human development journey. An invitation to follow Jesus may incentivize conversion, but often that decision comes through multiple spiritual encounters, as maturation develops throughout the seasons of life. Paul's instruction to the Corinthians leaders,

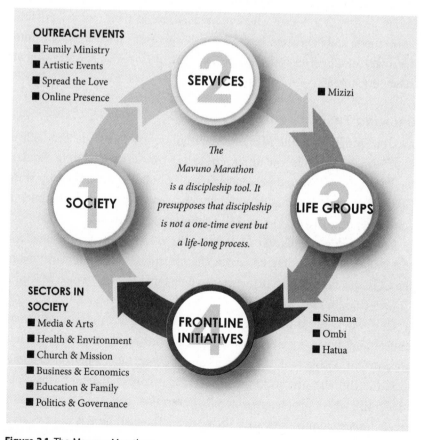

Figure 3.1. The Mavuno Marathon

"I planted the seed, Apollos watered it, but God has been making it grow" (1 Cor 3:6), presumes multiseasonal faith encounters. The Mavuno Marathon is therefore a realistic attempt to take the need for transformation of the whole person in the ordinary life cycle seriously. It assumes that effective discipleship is not a series of incidental, random actions following a spontaneous act of preaching and conversion.

If millennials have been estranged from a traditional understanding of church life, there is also the possibility that they haveno idea where to start to rebuild a relationship with God. But guided and supported in community, they can grow into faith-filled followers of Christ. The ministry and presence of the Holy Spirit is expected at every stage, working through leaders who are equipped for each of these points—for instance, in evangelism, healing prayer, restoring compassion, or building community. For the church leadership, the key is to locate where individuals are in their journey of faith, affirm them, and help them keep growing "with ever-increasing glory" into the image of Christ (2 Cor 3:18) in the body of Christ as it is growing at Mavuno Church.

GROWING THROUGH THE MARATHON

As seen in figure 3.1, the Mavuno Marathon journey is visualized as five steps from (1) complacent in society to (2) consumer attending Sunday services to (3) connected person consciously building a relationship with God and the church community and finding their purpose to (4) committed convert, and finally to (5) compelled follower of Christ.

Reaching the complacent in society. The complacent stage recognizes that society is now indifferent about church and has little familiarity with the Christian faith. So the first step is to help build interest, which Mavuno Church does in creative ways.

One way is to go to where people are and speak in a language they understand. If someone thinks the church is boring or irrelevant, or they are outright hostile to it, the church cannot expect such a person to come to it; the church must go to this person. So, the first stage of outreach is to identify where people are—literally in terms of physical location—and create honest connections with them there. The goal here is not to carry out evangelism; millennials can detect sales-type evangelism a mile away and will usually build up walls when they sense dishonesty. For its own context, Mavuno chose to build relationships across South C first. One example was to frequent nightclubs and hold entertaining events that engaged club patrons. A famous event in the early days of Mavuno was dubbed "Live @The Village" and was held at the Carnivore nightclub. Kanjii Mbugua would lead a team in performing Afro-neo soul music, a lyrical fusion of Nairobi urban storytelling and American R & B rhythms. Eventually, they would identify themselves and invite club patrons to check out Mavuno Church.

Reaching out to people at the complacent stage, Mavuno found that "Christianese" was not intelligible to these estranged millennials. Connecting with them meant speaking through mediums to which they were connected. Early on, Mavuno Church actively engaged through most social-media platforms: Twitter, Facebook, YouTube, Vimeo, blogs, and a website. Mavuno's sermons are posted on an open-access YouTube channel and streamed live on Vimeo. A Twitter hashtag marks Mavuno's 140-character sound bites, including its tweets during sermons or church events. Regular weekly updates on events in the church are posted on the church's Facebook page and a Flickr account displays its photos. Pastors encourage congregants to post personal responses and stories of transformation on the church's blogs, which include *Blog.Mavuno, Mizizi, Greatness Now,* and *Pastor Linda's Blog.* Open to the wider world, these channels are part of an outreach strategy that tells society that Mavuno Church is a cool place to belong. They also serve a double purpose of building community for regular Mavunites.

While Christian radio stations have been a popular means of sharing faith with the wider public, Mavuno does not own a radio station or even run a regular program on Christian radio. Muriithi's argument against it is that Christian radio speaks to an already Christianized demographic and does so with insider Christian language. So, in addition to their social-media presence, Mavuno church pastors often appear in primetime secular radio, not because they solicit the prime time, but because Mavuno sermons often engage controversial topics that create a buzz around the city, resulting in invitations to address such hot topics in the public domain. The pastors' approach to such invitations is not to "preach" per se but to infuse main-stream media with wholesome, society-positive conversations.

For Muriithi the use of technological tools to "reach a sight and sound generation" is a shift from a static text to a dynamic use of multiple platforms in a society that now uses these various human senses—sight, sound, touch, smell, taste. This shift from text-based reading and communication to the more epigrammatic media of sound bites, videos, and images does not nec-essarily mean the long forms are irrelevant. The short span of most of these media is more than compensated for by more frequent exposure to these new media. Through social media, Christians actually have more frequent access to a variety of Christian material, such as music, Scripture, video, and instant messages. At any rate, in the Mavuno Marathon the use of social media is an entry point to start conversation, but there are further steps.

Another creative effort at building bridges with the millennial world is to facilitate the formation of life-changing relationships. Mavuno Church's early surveys showed a major need for relational guidance within the millennial demographic. So in addition to the fun outreach events, Mavuno designed two courses intended to address life issues, the NDOA (Swahili for "marriage") and LEA (Swahili for "parenting") curriculums for families. NDOA, a ten-week group experience, was designed for couples in different stages of the marriage relationship who are seeking to grow in that relation-ship. Some are intending to get married, some are already living in a customary marriage, some are cohabiting, some are already legally married, and some are in conflict and coming for counsel. This course teaches essential biblical and social knowledge about marriage, designed in such a way as to help people navigate real issues. The experiential material is shaped around daily concerns on all kinds of relational issues. NDOA has led to the restoration of marriages where couples were on the verge of divorce. LEA is a parenting class whose participants are also drawn from the troubled child-raising territory within the wider society. It takes the same approach as NDOA, focusing on children, parents, and the multiple influences of work, school, television, media, and peers.

NDOA and LEA are seen as outreach curricula because participants are not required to have prior church experience in order to benefit from them. Mavuno outreach teams will go to gated residential estates where young couples are to be found, identify and respond to other specific needs in that residence, and engage in conversations that lead to class invitations. These events are planned by volunteer teams that are familiar with the neighborhoods and therefore already have a rapport. Pastoral staff comes along to lend support to volunteers. For example, in one residence, a child had a bad household accident while in the care of a nanny. Within weeks of this incident, Mavuno members in this residence mobilized a team of volunteers to run a well-attended household "clinic." They trained participants on first aid, culinary skills, and neighborhood-watch security. At the end of the class, thirty-seven people who had not been to Mavuno signed up for further classes, such as NDOA, LEA, and Mizizi.

Mavuno outreach teams frequently come up with such creative ways to go where people are, including high schools and college weekend visits. These are designed around entertainment to give the young people an avenue to expend energy in dance and creative expression, but speakers will address specific school or youth issues, including relationships, mentoring, and career development, to build foundations before the youth hit the uneasy young-adult years. Within the lower income settlements, football tournaments, games, and life-skill trainings are designed to engage the youth who are from less privileged families and would ordinarily just loaf in the streets. Because most of these activities are initiated within existing friendship networks, the community building goes beyond Sunday activity. Outreach therefore becomes about creating a space for friendships, strengthening families, and lessening isolation. In turn, this has also become an opportunity for young interns at Mavuno Church to hone their leadership skills.

Catering to the consumer within the church. At Mavuno Church it is understood that the person who comes out of the complacent society starts by casually attending church on Sundays. This person is a consumer. This stage affirms that they in fact are coming to church mainly because the church is meeting a certain need they have. Quite often those who come as first-time visitors are brought by a friend or heard about Mavuno through social media. While the goal of the first stage is to get the person into church, the goal of the consumer stage is to lower their defenses and open them up to spiritual conversation. This person is reached in the welcoming of first-time visitors, the choice of worship music, the quality of community time, the use of artistic props and media, as well as in the delivery of an engaging sermon.

The accommodation of a person who attends church as a consumer is seen to be counterintuitive to "real" Christianity. Consumer Christianity, some might say, employs methods that appeal to worldly desires, such as music, language, affective worship, and use of technology. Further, the use of business principles to run the organizational structures of church and the outreach methods to attract more people are seen to be ungodly. But in the Mavuno Marathon the consumer stage is simply an acknowledgment that in a world in which everything else is defined by the value it brings to the individual, especially the millennial, personal interest even in the choice of a church is inevitable. In the past there was a high degree of consensus on religious values, sites, and language to accompany the norms of group conformity. Words, symbols, morality, and worldview had a self-evident quality based on cognitive and normative assumptions that were dependent on widely accepted social conventions. There were recognizable geographical boundaries that defined one's religion or even denomination.

That is no longer the case. Most people are raised with little or no orientation toward the Bible. The stories, doctrinal teachings, and rituals of the church make very little sense to those outside the church. With the absence of the sacred canopy, rudiments of the Christian faith are foreign to the person coming to church as a beginner, so the task is one of translation rather than old-style liturgical re-education. People first need help to "get it" before they can be expected to connect. Second, in a metropolitan context that provides many options, including both partying over a weekend and participating in worship, individuals will consider what is in their best interest over against the inconveniences. Long before people act altruistically toward others, their actions are initially preceded by the question, "What is in it for me?" One might attract a person to church for a single event, but cost-benefit calculations underlie their decision to keep coming subsequently. Eventually this motivation should shift—and, as we will see, is designed to shift in the Mavuno Marathon—but at the entry point it does not help to ignore the fact that choice, convenience, and value have a lot to do with why anyone would wake up on a Sunday morning to go to church in a city offering other options.

The Mavuno Church Sunday service is therefore designed to create familiarity, appeal, and connection. Worship connects with what is familiar. In the early days of Mavuno, the music team would write Christian lyrics to popular secular songs and sing these during worship. They also sang the music of artists who bridged popular culture (see chapter five). Another connection point is community talk time in everyday language, which is both entertaining and informative. Afterward, visitors are invited to an easily accessible and tasteful visitor's lounge, where they continue this community connection. Here a volunteer welcomes and gives a five-minute spiel about the church, introduces some pastors, and invites questions. This icebreaker is usually followed up by phone calls and emails to link the person to more community life.

The sermon acts as another connection to the consumer. This is where it gets interesting. The sermon speaks to the whole community, yet in the design and the delivery, the intention is that visitors will hear God speak to them. The content can be deeply communal, reenact biblical stories, and give a missional challenge. What is crucial is to create curiosity for the person exploring church. A first-time visitor hears a sermon through nuance in communication and the relational accessibility of the preaching pastor. The support props, such as decor, media-shout presentations, and catchy takeaway lines are as important as what is said. To make sermons simultaneously accessible to the first-time visitor and meaningful to the regular church attender, a lot of preparation work is done in determining the content, form, method of delivery, and outcomes. Mavuno has a whole research department in charge of sermons and other curriculum to give due attention to all these aspects of any message that is delivered from the pulpit.

Discipling the connected in a core catechism class. The end goal of the Sunday services is to get the consumer to become connected to the life of the church. Mizizi is the catechism or discipleship class set up to build and reinforce three essential connections. As discussed earlier in this chapter, Mizizi emerged out of an experiment, so the course manual is beguilingly simple. It is arranged in readings for five days a week for ten weeks; each day's reading can take up to twenty minutes to complete. However, there is nothing simplistic about this course. It is designed as an overall experience of content that carefully thinks through issues that are significant to African millennials. The extra-class experiences—the facilitation process, which has a separate manual, and the group experience—work together to complete the encounter. In the introduction Muriithi states that Mizizi "is tailor made to help you grow deep roots for your Christian faith, to be the kind of Christian who experiences God daily and whose faith has long-term impact." The Mizizi blog on the Mavuno website explains that "Mizizi creates the environment that allows people to know and experience God's power to transform." This transforming experience consists of three connections—with God, community, and one's purpose.

The first three weeks of the Mizizi class are about how one begins a relationship with God. It starts by looking at common misconceptions from daily occurrences that a Kenyan millennial would have about God. For example, there are those who have an image of God as a "traffic policeman." This god detachedly patrols streets, unimpressed with good deeds, and indifferent to law-abiding citizens, but the minute he catches a little error, he is punitively unforgiving until one pays all dues to the law. Another caricature is of God as a VIP (very important person) in a corporate, top-corner office. This sort of god is so busy doing important things in his conglomerate realm that he is not interested in a nondescript individual. The other image is of God as an aging grandparent whom one visits and talks to regularly but only about inane things. Such a god, a remnant of a past era, is out of touch with reality. These are just a few of the evocative deconstructions in the Mizizi manual.

Day two of the Mizizi manual starts to disarm such misplaced views of God by examining the biblical character of God. God is the master designer who created humans for a relationship. He is interested and loves human beings. This day cites Genesis 1–2, Psalm 139, and Ephesians 2:10—all Scriptures that point to a God who is profoundly thoughtful in the way he created human beings and in his personal interest and purposeful actions to guide them. The third day looks at the human problem of separation, which has resulted in distorted images of God, then to points human flight from or fight with God. The consequences of separation are shown as several kinds of death: spiritual death, soul death, physical death, societal death, and environmental degradation. Day four presents the good news of the cross of Christ. The cross of Christ is presented as the bridge to forgiveness and relationship with God. Repentance, confession, and surrender to the lordship of Christ is invited, with an emphasis on the power of the cross to liberate the conscience and transform the life. This is facilitated by a personal decision to follow Christ, after which the new convert is encouraged to go through baptism by immersion (which takes place at the end of a Mizizi season). Another day's study highlights how Satan keeps individuals from a relationship with God. The devil accuses one as too much of a sinner, too ordinary to achieve anything good, too insignificant for God to care, and so on. Each accusation is countered by a positive affirmation from Scripture, such as that one is accepted as a child of God (Jn 1:12), bought at a price through the sacrifice of Christ (1 Cor 6:19-20), forgiven all sins (Col 1:14), and made to be salt and light in the world and therefore able to make a difference (Mt 5:13-14). The reading ends by inviting the individual to examine and counter the lies of the enemy with relevant Scriptures and faith-based promises.

Assuming that one has made the choice to follow, the second week of Mizizi is about learning to hear God through devotional practices, which include reading the Bible daily, cultivating a lifestyle of consistent prayer, listening to the wise counsel of other believers, and listening to God's instructions through life's circumstances, creation, and supernatural means. Each day's readings are supported by questions that help to personalize the lesson and the weekly group experience.

From here, Mizizi explores the cost of being a believer. Reorienting repentance from guilt and remorse toward surrender, one is invited to let God be the "new manager" of their affairs. Common excuses, such as the need to fix one's problems first or accumulate enough "capital" (that is, be good enough), are challenged and countered with Scripture that affirms God's commitment. The unbeliever is invited to begin the lifetime journey toward Christlikeness: "Day by day as we submit ourselves to Christ we will find the issues we struggled with in the past are no longer as daunting, and as we win victory over them we will find other challenges awaiting us. The saying, 'I'm not yet what I'd like to be, but I'm surely not what I used to be,' will continue to be true every year."[2] At some point participants are invited to take an action that signifies surrender. One example is to sign a symbolic "Deed of Ownership" over to the Lord with the witness of a friend (see figure 3.2).

---

[2] Wanjau, *Mizizi*, 38.

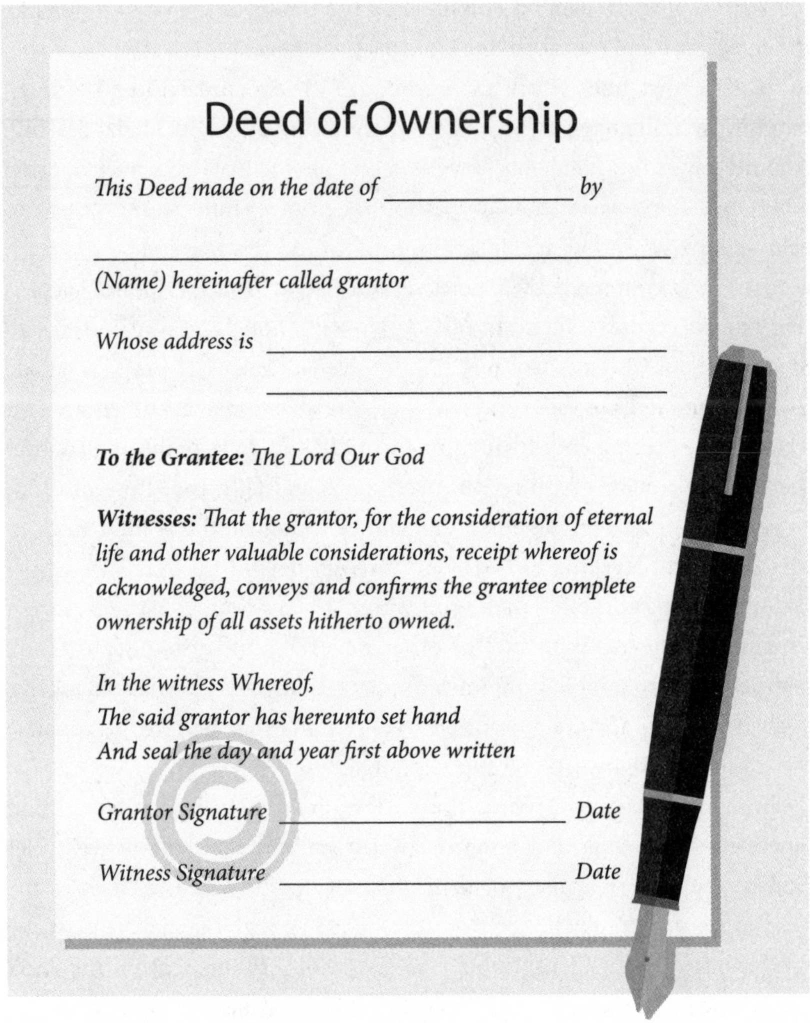

Deed of Ownership

This Deed made on the date of _____ *by*

_____

(Name) hereinafter called grantor

Whose address is _____

_____

To the Grantee: *The Lord Our God*

Witnesses: *That the grantor, for the consideration of eternal life and other valuable considerations, receipt whereof is acknowledged, conveys and confirms the grantee complete ownership of all assets hitherto owned.*

In the witness Whereof,
The said grantor has hereunto set hand
And seal the day and year first above written

Grantor Signature _____ *Date*

Witness Signature _____ *Date*

Figure 3.2. Mizizi Deed of Ownership

The second connection is with community. Mizizi is as much an experience of building community as it is a spiritual discovery course. Group experiences are intended to build relationships. On the surface, millennials come to class looking polished under a cool exterior or having a loud, boisterous presence. But underneath are a variety of personal life stories, perhaps involving broken families of origin, betrayal and hurt from significant others, financial difficulties, work stresses, struggles with substance abuse, and absence of personal direction.

One goal of Mizizi is therefore to remove the masks so that participants realize that everyone has issues. Spontaneous outdoor events, class games, and food time are thus not incidental to the main "spiritual life" of a Mizizi class. These are structured to create spaces where friendship becomes the key to meaningful class conversation. Another way to build friendships is to help people serve together. Encounter with those who are less fortunate is usually a powerful way to reorient how people see their own problems. A class might visit a children's home, prison, hospital, or rural village. The groups are given initial guidance and encouragement on these visits, but in the end they choose where they want to engage because group ownership of an initiative is important. By week five, these friendships are strong. This is when the Mizizi lesson focuses on helping class participants understand Christ's vision for the community as a body. As per 1 Corinthians 12, those who belong to Christ are members of one body, connected to each other and to Christ. Church is a place to love God through others, to serve the body of Christ, and to belong as one loved by God and by others that love God.

The third connection in Mizizi is with a God-given purpose. For most postcollege adults, inability to achieve dreams is a major setback that often leads to a sense of victimization by society and drifting into egocentric practices. With a growing awareness that as an educated generation they actually have choices and God-given resourcefulness, participants in Mizizi learn that life is more than personal dreams. One's success is tied to living for a transcendent cause beyond the self. This is linked to serving others, spreading goodness, and pursuing whatever brings God's glory into the world. In week six Mizizi discusses God's concern for the world and for the lost. Focus on God's mission goes beyond sharing faith individually. Conversations expand toward God's mission in the world. God expects believers to be resourceful, to help the less fortunate, to address problems such as bad leadership, conflict, poverty, and corruption, and to transform the troubled arenas of society. Here Muriithi cites the prototypical evangelical document, the Lausanne Covenant: "God wants his whole church to take the whole gospel to the whole world." He also quotes Genesis 12, where God blessed Abraham so that he would become a blessing to the world. In this time in history, God's intention is to bless the whole world through the church. Those attending Mavuno are reminded that even when they have troubled families of origin, they are in fact the privileged class of society because they have an education, which opens up possibilities of choice, so they are to influence society.

By week nine Mizizi wraps up the theme of mission by helping every person identify their missional toolkit. This is traced through the acronym SHAPE: Spiritual gifts (S) are a complement to one's identity as God's child. Heart (H) reflects one's deepest longings, commitments, or fears (because fears can hold one back from commitment). The question "What do you have a heart for?" seeks what participants are passionate about, what energizes them, and it points to the area of society or community that they should seek to transform with their gifts and skills. Abilities (A) are what one is naturally good at, such as dancing, writing, science, administering, sports, and so on. Participants are encouraged to cultivate their abilities and excel in them. Personality (P) is the center from which one makes life decisions and relational choices. This affects what they do with their spiritual gifts and abilities. One is challenged to be aware of their personality. Experience (E) is what one has experienced and how it affects the rest of one's SHAPE. Awareness of one's SHAPE toolkit is key to discovering and living out one's purpose and therefore becoming a fearless influencer of society.

Pursuit of purpose is a central emphasis in Mizizi. The word *purpose* has acquired currency about a wide range of endeavors, from running a profitable business to having a fulfilling career to embracing meaningful life responsibilities. Mavuno's emphasis was born of discernment of reality for Mike and Makena. In the African past, children were socialized into fixed roles through predictable stages and were then initiated into those roles at appropriate times. With modern education, socialization has been left to schools, which in turn focuses on a fixed curriculum designed to prepare for a perceived job market. The school environment is supposed to facilitate maturation through extracurricular activities. However, except for those in private schools, the psychological strains of a dysfunctional system of education and troubled family backgrounds send most of the postschool young adults into the world unsure of their place in life. Then the urban social crowd and professional pressure diminishes clarity of life's direction. Young adults will move through shifting definitions of identity, profession, and relationships with little sense of cohesion, thus creating a personal psychological predicament. Encouraging them to discover and pursue their purpose is about helping them focus their quest by understanding their world, understanding and mastering themselves, cultivating a value system, building relationships, and developing the personal disciplines needed to achieve God-given potential. All this comes full-circle through the lessons learned in Mizizi, other curriculums in Life groups, and sermons that flesh out these issues.

The committed in the church community. Following the complacent, consumer, and connection steps, the next stage in the Mavuno Marathon is the committed person. By now the person is well known in a small, solid community formed in Mizizi. The group cultivates their identity within the larger church community that is somehow also a movement. Three levels of commitment are refined.

One level is to participate in a life group. The Mizizi class turns into a group for life, commissioned to pursue the three As: association, accountability, and application. In *association*, group members to relate to one another around life in its breadth as a new kind of kinship. In *application*, members study Scripture together and apply it to specific situations. They are encouraged to discuss and apply Mavuno's Sunday sermons but may choose something different. *Accountability* is about asking one another about known areas of growth; strengthening through prayer, confession, and forgiveness; and extending care. Here is where further mending of the torn social fabric takes place. In a small group people discover their life experiences are similar to those of others. Paradox, difficulties, struggle, and grief become shared sources of growth. Group life also includes presence in ceremonies that reinforce life transitions, such as baptisms, child dedications, weddings, and funerals. Groups also serve together, such as in a neighborhood need, local outreach, and or international mission trip.

In life groups there is also a commitment to mature in faith. While Mizizi covers a lot of ground, ten weeks is not enough time for a quality exploration of discipleship. Muriithi's pastoral colleagues designed educational courses to address specifics of the African young adult life-world. Simama (from the Swahili for "stand") looks to the crisis type of personal baggage acquired from families of origin, adverse lifestyle choices, and social instabilities. Simama was developed by Muriithi's wife, Carol, a psychologist with two graduate degrees in theology. After she conducted numerous individual counseling sessions with young adults, she determined that healing was more effective through group ministry. Charismatic prayer and anointing on Sundays does lead to some release, but recovery happens in community support. In designing Simama to address problems of the Nairobi urbanite, she combines insight from traditional African wisdom, Scripture, and developmental psychology.

NDOA similarly addresses issues in the context of making and raising a family. While the material is designed to appeal even to those who are not believers, key learning points address family challenges, work roles, personalities, family roles, marital expectations, in-laws, and outlaws. The course considers how to understand each other, build expectations in a marriage, break negative habits and adopt good ones, nurture stages of marriage, manage family finances, build communication, and so on. LEA is the parenting curriculum for young parents. Ombi (Swahili for "prayer"), written by Simon Mbevi, who was once a pastor at Mavuno, is a curriculum for life groups about how to pray for their families, workplaces, and country. Hatua (Swahili for "step") was written by Linda Ochola, a theologian with a specialty in the Old Testament. She has served as an executive and leadership-development pastor. In Hatua she trains Mavuno members to challenge the dysfunctional social and political world through study of the Old Testament.

Together these are known as the Marathon classes. They all run concurrently over a season of ten weeks, with three seasons per year, according to the church's annual calendar. Each class has its own cohort of trainers, coaches, facilitators, scheduled events, meeting venues, retreats, and special activities.

Another level of commitment is supporting the vision of the church financially. Just like every other subject, millennials handle financial matters like a patchwork of broken telephone lines, so to speak. Much of the existing education system does not teach about life in any substantial way, whether family, work, or money. The eighth week of Mizizi therefore addresses this thorny question, focusing on how one should steward

God-entrusted resources, how to get out of debt, save up for the future, be a resource for kingdom work, and meet the needs of others. Teaching about finances is a core aspect of the annual preaching calendar. Each year Muriithi addresses a wide variety of issues that relate finances to lifestyle in the present and the future, to faith commitment, and to participation in God's mission.

Three principles of successful money management emerge out of Muriithi's teaching in Mizizi and from sermons. His first money principle is ownership, that God is the creator, source, and owner of all wealth; those who have it are intended to be stewards, as seen in Jesus' many parables about money. God entrusts resources to people according to their ability and takes them away from those who manage them badly. Christians are to spend and invest wisely on God's behalf. The second is the management principle. When Christians take good care of wealth, talents, and resources that God has given, they become recipients of more blessings, including intangible blessings like joy, purpose, fulfillment, and contentment, the "true riches of heaven." Management includes giving tithes and offerings, helping the poor, and caring for parents. Muriithi also encourages paying taxes to government as part of God's expectations of Christians. The third money principle is saving—setting aside income for the future. He recommends a budget as an essential tool for good management of God's resources.

Mavuno is a financially successful church. Funds are raised primarily through tithes and offerings and are used to meet ministry, staff, and administrative costs; rent; and capital development of the permanent property. To stay above board and demonstrate good stewardship to the congregation, financial affairs are run by professional accountants, regulated by strictures of accounting, including procedural austerity on accounting of self-funding events. The meticulous design of the system leaves no room for financial impropriety. Accounts are audited annually by business professionals, and a government audit is carried out every three years.

The third mark of commitment to the vision is serving in the church. As participants in Mizizi discover their spiritual gifts, they are encouraged to serve in some capacity, regardless of their spiritual maturity. The Marathon classes—Mizizi, Simama, Ombi, Hatua—require hundreds of facilitators, administrators, and spiritually mature coaches. All these are recruited, trained, and developed within the departments of the Marathon. Serving is a way of developing the priesthood of believers—by allowing them to discover and use their SHAPE. In service the goal is not expertise. If one does not feel they have spiritual or technical qualifications, they serve under a qualified leader and thereby receive mentoring. The pastoral teams and coaches help to discern appropriate levels of spiritual and technical responsibility. Muriithi's rationale for challenging every member of Mavuno to serve is to call out servant leaders, train them to become fearless influencers, help them grow closer to God and the community, and reinforce the pursuit of purpose.

Serving is also the opportunity to become a decision maker in the congregation. Volunteers are known as "associates" and are considered leaders and full members of the church. Associates have gone through Mizizi and therefore know the church's DNA, have accountability through a life group, and are growing in new ministry skills. Twice a year all service teams congregate for "leaders' days," the equivalent of the annual general meeting in older churches. A leaders' day in the early part of the year creates space to report on the ministries, cast vision for the year, and enlist prayer and commitment. The second leaders' day later in the year celebrates the year and envisions further ahead. Service teams are departmentally trained by pastoral staff, and the annual Fearless Conference brings all teams together for an intense, three-day, inspirational event, to which leaders from other churches are also invited.

Service teams are recognized and strengthened through a month-long celebration sermon series every November, culminating in an awards ceremony, called the "Fearless Awards," to recognize outstanding diligence among volunteers. Each department showcases their Marathon division. This in turn helps develops a greater integration among teams. As with everything that Mavuno Church does, intentional design is central to the awards idea, so that the key message is not lost in the detail. For instance, the token awards are themselves a more symbolic feature rather than preferential treatment of particular volunteers. The showcase of the entire cohort of volunteers is what matters most. Fearless Awards categories are diverse and sometimes newly invented as ministry teams diversify their initiatives. Awards include team leader of the year, servant leader, societal impact leader, mentor of the year, risk taker, best team, young achievers among the teens and children, and so on. November is one of the most exciting months at Mavuno.

All these Marathon classes, gatherings, and community events simultaneously serve to build a strong community. Mavuno events have an identifiable Mavuno way of doing things, a "Mavuno culture DNA," which has the core values of relevance, excellence, authenticity, and passion. *Relevance* means that Mavuno structures ministry around the millennial demographic. Commitment to relevance informs the preaching calendar and sermon preparation, the choice of music, and the service artistry with the intention of creating space for multiple levels of participation and growth, use of different spiritual gifts, and modeling of how fearless influence can be extended beyond church. *Excellence* is modeled by the staff team through an overall organizational culture of professionalism and commitment to utilize all the spiritual gifts and material resources well, as good stewards of all that God makes available. The rationale is based on the fact of God's admiration of everything he created and declared, "It is good." *Authenticity* points to a learning community, modeled through candid and unaffected conversation in curricular experiences, preaching, and leadership roles. Hence, testimonies in church, on blogs, in magazines, and at events are similarly candid. *Passion* is initially modeled by those in the lead, but a young crowd quickly catches enthusiasm when they find something meaningful. Passion bonds with excellence, authenticity, and relevance as the DNA of events, seen in attendance and group branding, as well as in responses to more specific calls by the pastors.

Sending the compelled into society. The final step of the Marathon is to become one of the compelled. Over time individuals progress through the Marathon track with increasing spiritual maturity, service experience, and commitment to Christ and community. The *compelled* know their SHAPE. More importantly, they should be able to identify themselves as part of a movement engaged in God's mission in the world. They see their work, family, and society at large as places where they can become agents of transformation. They pray regularly for the church, society, and nation, give sacrificially of time and resources and apply whatever they are learning at Mavuno in their arena of influence. They are driven to make a significant difference because of their faith. Such a compelled person is therefore one who, while remaining vitally connected to the rest of the life of the church, embraces Mavuno's mission of "turning ordinary people into fearless influencers of society" in a personal way.

The formation of a "fearless influencer" is described by each word of this mission statement. "Turning" means that Mavuno is not about information (great sermons and curriculum) or entertainment (great services and events), although these are integrally connected to the journey of continuous transformation. Mavuno is about life change reflected in all of one's work and life relationships over the course of time. "Ordinary people" means that Mavuno appreciates the background of a society that has experienced deep volatility. Everybody comes in with baggage that needs to be dealt with. Naming the ordinariness creates a readiness to navigate it with others who are similarly ordinary. Quite often in Marathon classes people will say, "I thought I was the only one struggling with this problem." "Into fearless influencers of society" means that after a person has been coming to Mavuno for a while, they are well on their journey into fearless influence. The gospel has not only liberated the person, it has instilled a sense of purpose and added eternal significance to their aspirations. They have a desire to become a transforming influence on society, and as movement they are an army of fearless influencers in the world.

There is even a creed, written by Tina Nduba, one of the earliest Mizizi participants, that outlines this fearless influence:

I am a Fearless Influencer . . .
My past is forgiven, my future is secure
My present is not for me, but for the one who set me free
The die has been cast, I have stepped over the line
No more prayer-less living, cheap giving & selfish dreaming
I am part of the change; I will not hesitate to serve
I will gladly pay the cost, contagiously spreading His love,
Playing my role on the dream team, the Mavuno family
Until all Africa is changed, every sector of society
I align myself to God's purpose, I will be who He calls me to be
I agree to be shaped & molded, through His word and through His family

Until my will and His will fully agree
And I become fully the influencer that I was created to be
I am a Fearless Influencer.

In the previous chapter I talked about the societal alienation that has affected the millennial generation as it has come of age. Christian tradition has epitomized metaphorical homelessness through the story of the prodigal son. The story tends to gain its greatest significance in the analogy of the son who walked away. But the problem is not merely with the rebellious son who leaves the sacred canopy. It is the entire narrative of the father, the sons, and their worlds that is emblematic of alienation. The conditions of social change in the world today, as would have been the case in Jesus' time, suggest that there are multiple layers under which modern individuals are buried before they turn prodigal. By the time rebellion—drunkenness, promiscuous living, broken relationships—becomes apparent there are already layers of family, societal, communal, and structural issues. Once the whole social fabric is broken, mending it requires a grasp of the extent to which everyone is linked to dysfunction. The Mavuno Marathon is therefore more than a plan to get the millennials back into church; it is a plan to get the individual, group, community, and movement to be part and parcel of restoring African society to wholeness through the transforming power of the gospel.

The Mavuno Marathon is a journey that takes ordinary people out of society and walks them through a transforming experience. The compelled stage is the point at which a Mavuno person is fully aware that God is at work in the world and that God has called people to join in that work to bring the redeeming influence to all human institutions and all created order. So while the goal is not necessarily to Christianize, it is to resource those places with action and thinking that reflects an awareness that God is at work everywhere and that redeemed humanity is in partnership with God. Every realm of human activity is the arena of God's mission, but for clarity, Muriithi has classified society into six sectors that need fundamental transformation: media and arts, family and education, business and economy, politics and governance, and church and mission.

Every year Muriithi preaches a two-month long sermon series on each of these sectors, working through the detail of the current national and regional conditions, interviewing Mavuno members who are working in them, and looking at practical ways Christians can engage. While the conceptualization of each sector is always a work in progress, these sermon series have helped congregation members see mission as far more than preaching and converting people. It is about integrally approaching what one is educated, trained, qualified, empowered, and even salaried to do in ordinary, day-to-day life as part of their service to God and witness to the world.

The clearest expression of the compelled person is that they may start, or help to start, a *frontline initiative* that addresses specific issues in any of the above sectors. The ownership, that is, the vision, funding, and leadership structures, of a frontline initiative belongs with the person that feels so compelled. However, Mavuno Church is always the initial family where a compelled member shares his or her vision and mobilizes startup resources and supporters. A person's life group is often that first base, and the departments may be involved in mobilization and networking other life groups, volunteers, and corporate companies or partner churches to support the initiative. I will discuss some of these initiatives in chapter five.

In chapter two I discussed the background conditions that would inform how Mavuno Church framed its message. This chapter has painted a more complete picture of the Mavuno Marathon, showing the logic and the steps of moving from indifference to participation. The next task is to connect all this thinking and action to leadership. Chapter four will begin with the formation process of the senior pastor, then move on to the structures around which the Marathon has taken shape and the learning curve that has shaped the leaders.

4

. . . .

Muriithi Wanjau

Leading Change

FORMATION OF A LEADER

When we consider pastors of megachurches, we tend to see the charismatic personality in the mature congregation. However, to understand them, their message, and their influence on a particular demographic, we need to discern how their personal biographies link with social volatility in wider society and how others resonate with the constellation of experiences embodied in them. If one listens to megachurch pastors long enough, one realizes that not only do they tell a lot of personal stories, they also do not deviate too far from a selective narrative of how the gospel is the solution to the wider social crisis. That is the clue and cue to their message, method, and influence on those they lead. What is popularly seen as charisma, "the man or woman of the moment," is only part of a longer formation process that includes intellectual ability and a demonstrable educational history. A conversion narrative in young adulthood and providential encounters with older, often unsung, heroes converges with the possibilities provided by education to make sense of the larger crisis and the missional call they discern as their own.[1]

This is certainly the case for Muriithi Wanjau, who steered Mavuno Church toward specifically defined change. Born in 1970, his parents were employed by the government in a time when a career in civil service was

---

[1]See Wanjiru Gitau, "Formation of African Christian Leaders: Patterns from ALS Data," in *African Christian Leadership: Realities, Opportunities, and Impact*, ed. Robert J. Priest and Kirimi Barine (Maryknoll, NY: Orbis Books, 2017).

part of the success of the immediate postcolonial generation. Yet the hopes of the Uhuru generation would fizzle by the end of the 1970s and through the 1980s.

Colonial rule ended in 1963. After independence, President Jomo Kenyatta enthusiastically galvanized the country through a credo of collective unity, *Harambee*, and with the help of much aid from Western governments (as with the rest of the Africa), he began an ambitious program to eradicate disease, poverty, and ignorance. Initially, Kenya was seen as a developmental success. However, the new nation maintained the hegemony of the colonial order, designed to benefit the elite and those in power. Plans to build societal consensus and economic success lacked corresponding structures to unite disparate ethnic groups. In the late 1960s, Jomo Kenyatta fell out with opposition leaders, especially Jaramogi Oginga from the Luo community. Kenyatta's power became centralized among those ethnically closest to him, and the clout isolated other communities. Then in the 1970s, a crisis in the OPEC (oil producing and exporting) countries reverberated across other commodity prices. Kenya's chief exports of coffee and tea lost market value. In the 1980s the situation deteriorated quickly as Western donors realized that foreign aid was not incentivizing economic growth in African countries. The International Monetary Fund (IMF) and the World Bank compelled African nations to effect structural adjustment (SAPs) and to cut back on civil service and public spending. But the conditions that could incentivize a private sector were missing. For instance, the education system had not been designed to encourage creative thinking; the one-party system of politics skewed the sharing of national resources toward the elite; and global commodity markets favored Western economies. Throughout the 1980s Kenya functioned as an informal state in which the formal administrative structures of a democracy were bypassed in favor of patrimonial interests in the ever-shrinking kitty of state resources. Whenever one needed a job or service in a civil office, the unofficial interview question was, "Whom do you know here?" Otherwise one gave a "little something" in exchange for service. To add insult to injury, an unknown disease, which we now know as HIV/AIDS, began to have a devastating impact, while the implosion of neighboring countries generated regional unease rather than an investment climate.

This was the kind of daily news that Muriithi grew up with. By the 1990s, in his young adult years, Kenya, like many African countries, seemed like a basket case. While he was a relatively sheltered middle-class kid, he would gain clarity about the crisis in the nation in the years he served and learned under Muriu at Nairobi Chapel. The link to his personal mission would then come in the transitional decade of the 2000s.

In his Christian life, Muriithi could identify with the biography of the conformers and adaptors discussed in chapter two. Although he grew up embracing the godly values of his parents, he did not expect to follow his father's midcareer calling to the pastorate in the Anglican Church. He detached from his parents' faith as a teenager. Soon after high school, his mother sent him to a Word of Life Camp, where he had a conversion experience. But that did not change him, and he continued to live as nominally as his rugby and clubbing buddies. In 1989 he began studies at the University of Nairobi. Within the first week, Muriu invited him and several others to a party for first-year students that had been organized at Nairobi Chapel. Subsequently, Muriu led him and other students to pursue a deeper faith and devised service opportunities to engage them. Muriithi's encounter with Nairobi Chapel and Muriu was his spiritual turning point.

When Muriithi completed university studies, Muriu recruited him, together with Carol, his girlfriend, to the internship. They married in 1994 while they served as pastoral trainees. In 1996 they left for theological education at the world-famous Fuller Theological Seminary and Azusa Pacific University in California. When they returned to Kenya in 2001, Muriithi was appointed as missions and church-planting pastor. He oversaw nineteen churches in low-income areas of the city. Most of these turned out to be learning experiences rather than successful churches, as they were not modeled on the Nairobi Chapel middle-class style. In 2004 Muriu took a sabbatical and left Muriithi and Janet Mutinda in charge. Then in 2005 Muriithi led his team of four other pastors and four hundred members to plant Mavuno. He led for two years without numerical success, but in 2008 they relocated to a more accessible location. Since they had built cultural capital during those two hidden years, the easy access at the drive-in cinema attracted young adults from all over the southwestern neighborhood. Mavuno Church grew from four hundred people in June 2008 to eighteen hundred by the end of the year. By 2010 they were averaging three thousand adults per weekend, a children's church of six hundred, and a teen service of four hundred at peak times.

In chapter three we saw how Mavuno articulated the message that helped postcollege millennials find their place in the world. In a world distraught by social change, the map of reality that the new leaders created is the key to understanding the leaders themselves. Muriithi's sense of challenges facing Africa, his motivation, and his ambition sprung out of his experience growing up in distressed times. He was determined to build a better life. As a young man, long before he encountered Nairobi Chapel, he was set on becoming a rich pharmacist. His intellectual acumen would have allowed him to succeed into an upper-middle-class lifestyle, were it not for Nairobi Chapel reorienting his life path. He went to Nairobi High School—back in the days when it was part of the Kenyan "Ivy League," along with Starehe Boys Centre—which only admitted the top percentile of students in the national exam system. He enrolled at the University of Nairobi, Kenya's premier research university, to study biochemistry, which again admitted only A students into science programs. In addition, he loved competitive sport and played rugby in high school and university. The touch of machismo on his social-media handles—such as "Greatness Now," which is the title for his blog, and "Life is not a rehearsal," the tagline for his blog—captures that gung-ho, go-getter spirit of his sports days.

Muriithi brought this intellectual and social charisma to his career in church. In chapter one I pointed out that Muriu took gutsy leadership risks in a time when pastors did not step out of the pious pastoral mode conventionally assigned to them. Yet he still functioned within the script traditionally assigned to a pastor. But his actions in the 1990s had the far-reaching consequences of awakening Muriithi's intellectually astute generation, which was a more prophetic outcome than Muriu's initial plan.

Conversely, Muriithi gradually recognized the precarious direction the country and continent were going, designed change, allied with his personal drive to succeed, and mentored others to think likewise. He was raised as a middle-class kid who felt the disillusionment of his parents' generation through two decades of national atrophy. Later, in the 2000s, he would read the same frustrations in a new key among postcollege young adults.

During his five years in America, he acutely internalized the denigrated status of Africa in the wider world.

Muriithi wanted to solve Africa.

"Change Africa or die trying" is the tagline that goes with Muriithi's Twitter handle. His pastoral success is not in spite of the intellect demonstrated by his personal educational biography and charisma. It is because of it. Muriithi's ability to mobilize a self-conscious, technologically connected generation comes from the fact that he is one of them, just steps ahead in age, exposure, and life experience. That proximity has an added advantage. Although intellectual acuity is essential to how he frames his message and leadership, to the regular young adult, his central appeal is his natural ability to show them that he genuinely resonates with their deepest concerns and is struggling to overcome the same limitations and find the same success. This comes through in his sermons: He starts with a revealing, personal, down-to-earth story. He dresses, lives, and drives like his audience. So do those who have learned leadership from him. And so the buzz spreads the "fictive" kinship of proximity, friendship, unaffected accessibility, and modest lifestyle, which attracts others, and the "village" widens into a large church. His first name, Muriithi, means "shepherd," which is completely coincidental but relevant to his pastoral career. (The name comes from his parent's lineage after the Kikuyu naming custom.)

Disciplined Mentoring

While intellectual acuity and personal drive helped crystallize his message, how he shaped leadership is linked to his disciplined mentoring by Muriu. Part of the reason that Muriu recruited graduates from public universities was that they brought a practical mindset to the task of ministry leadership. Those trained in theological programs tended to bring a largely pious attitude to church work. Muriu preferred to start with the rookie. He might later send a trainee to seminary to get their theological angles sharpened, but early on Muriu realized that if he recruited an intern who had a relationship with God and displayed personal integrity, he could teach them most aspects of leadership on the job and coach their spiritual journey through a wide variety of reading resources that he himself was reading. Muriithi summarizes three critical skills in which Muriu trained him and the other interns in their daily responsibilities: to think contextually, raise others and delegate, and solve problems.

To think and generate new ideas. First, Muriithi says that Muriu taught him how to think like an African in the late twentieth-century world. Looking back to the early to mid-1990s when he was Muriu's protégé, the large wave of global media was making a sweeping entry into Kenya. It particularly affected urban youth, who aped pop music sensations from America. The intellectual elite often decried this "crying shame of cultural capitulation" but did not have workable solutions for how to get youth to appreciate local cultures and restore their respect for ways of the elders.[2] In theological circles, the discourse was framed in terms of need for an inculturation theology in the churches. Theological thought leaders called for the revaluation and preservation of the African cultural past, the wisdom of the elders, and African identity and community values.

Muriu challenged his interns to learn to think in the first place, and second, to think of problems creatively and follow through with practical actions. For instance, he knew that university students would not come to the church to sing the beautiful old hymns. So he invited Muriithi and other students to form a band to lead worship, which was completely counterintuitive. He challenged them to introduce styles that mattered to their university friends. Muriithi and his band brought their guitars and drums. At the time, the Hosanna! Integrity label represented the hot new type of worship, so they played these songs to replace the hymns, much to the consternation of some remaining members of the old Nairobi Chapel. At that point this music deeply resonated with university students, so Muriu replaced the old church organ with keyboards, drums, electric and bass guitars, and the upbeat music.

As room for creativity and experimentation expanded, other forms of continuity with African tradition would emerge and renew the Nairobi Chapelites' sense of pride in being both urbane and African. For instance, Marcy Karianjahi, another intern turned pastor from the 1990s, led multiple choir troupes in writing music that blended folksy dance celebrations, complete with African-themed robes, with global contemporary tunes for

---

[2]See Kimani Njogu and Garnette Oluoch-Olunya, *Cultural Production and Social Change in Kenya: Building Bridges* (Kenya: Twaweza Communications, 2007).

a unique Nairobi Chapel audience. The mishmash of urbanized, traditional, artsy styles of dance with newly spreading global tunes created a distinctively Nairobi Chapel kind of music, again novel for its time, though no longer so with media diffusion today. Muhia Karianjahi, Marcy's husband, wrote a curriculum based on the traditional initiation ceremony as the "Rites of Passage Program" (ROPEs), an annual program for pubescent boys and girls to recover the traditional value of coaching them into young adulthood. ROPEs, still a signature program at Nairobi Chapel, takes preteen children through a year of training on their upcoming adulthood, then as a transition sends them off to a grueling week of camping with somewhat traditional counselors and special parental sessions. Another innovation was to recover traditional community accountability and support through small groups that came to be known as ekklesia groups. Among other things these groups banded together to raise money to support medical clinics in the slums.

Since all these are now familiar and almost acculturated forms in many middle-class churches in Kenya, it is easy to overlook how much they represented out-of-the-box thinking in the 1990s. At the time some of the creative experiments had Nairobi Chapel labeled as a cult by overly pious Christians from older churches, to warn the university community to stay away. Muriu stayed focused on inventing practical ways of encouraging the urbane students, and he found that once they were resourced to be creative, one creative act would lead to another. He was not fixated on reinventing fixed forms of African tradition. More important was that students, and later congregants and leaders, would see how the Bible's teachings connect with current problems, then link them with their own creative skills. Revalorization of any African form—such as cultural food habits, rituals of communal association, extravagant cultural dress, dance, rites of passage, and so on—was contingent on the situation, whether preaching a sermon, officiating a wedding, or helping in low-income quarters.

However, as with Muriu's learning-on-the-go leadership, whatever ideas he generated were not ready to take fixed form as a Nairobi Chapel "brand" (as Mavuno would early on create its own brand), perhaps because other contextual realities had not reached "the fullness of time." In the 1990s all programs of societal renewal hit a roadblock sooner or later. On the national scene, churches and politicians tried to bring about political change. Mainline churches allied with other religious traditions in the Ufungamano Initiative to change the constitution for better governance and redistribution of national resources. New political parties tried to unseat Moi. The crises of poverty and disease peaked in this decade too. Muriithi needed to take a break from all the intense growing under the driven Muriu to consolidate his learning through theological reflection. By the time he left to study at Fuller Theological Seminary, he deeply felt the impact of the country's seemingly intractable problems. To him the gospel had power to unleash change; however, at the time it wasn't clear how he would make this happen. Away from the powerful influence of his mentor, Fuller Theological Seminary gave him the opportunity to reflect on his experience in a much wider world.

When Muriithi and his team relocated to the South C area, the realities of the neglected 8-4-4 generation became the outline of a transforming vision, and their creative experiments birthed the Mavuno Marathon. For instance, the young crowd was in the night-clubs because those places gave them a semblance of connection—alternative community that was lacking in the otherwise routine pressures of urban life. Community was the primary need of Nairobi urbanites, but building it had to take into consideration different times, settings, and needs than it did in Nairobi Chapel days. Attracting millennials to church would mean more than classy drums and zingy guitars. Mavuno's worship director, Kanjii Mbugua, introduced a whole new genre of music, starting with the music of the "mutinous" Kirk Franklin, the African American gospel-music sensation, then rewriting Christian lyrics to Kenyan pop tunes, and later writing Christmas and Easter stories into Kenyan family dramas. The full significance of this shift will be discussed in chapter five, but suffice it to say here that simply figuring out musical styles would have extensive impact.

Another way to think creatively was to rebuild community for millennials. Through the ubiquitous FM stations, televisions, and social-media networks, young people were linked with more information than ever before. Yet these were not used as resources for knowledge and business creativity, because there weren't many models for how to use them productively. In the rambunctious nightclubs that they frequented, the young adults had the semblance of community, but by day they were hustling. The political process had no workable vision for the youth. The clientelist state of the 1990s had shifted into new hands when the Mwai Kibaki government came to power in 2003. Yet apart from political realignments and big-picture wheeling and dealing, the Kenya of the early 2000s barely had a blueprint of legitimate wealth creation, let alone the ability to encourage the ingenuity of the youth. Nairobi was expanding at a phenomenal rate, yet the gap between the rich and the poor was widening, and slum populations were also increasing. Families were haunted by greater rates of divorce, broken and single-parent homes, teenage pregnancies, and alcohol dependency. The second political liberation seemed to have fallen flat on its face.

How does one begin to transform such a world without being paralyzed by its acute pain? More than a spiritual space, Mavuno had to become an environment that would add value to the lives of the young. If anything was to attract them, it would have to be a genuine alternative to what they were getting in clubs. Conversations would have to be authentic, not theologically abstract. This is how the worship band ended up staging events in nightclubs. They also turned the church events into fun-based activities. In those early days, it was said that Mavuno knew how to have a good party, with food, DJs, syncopated music, synthesizers, full-glow stroboscopic lighting effects—the works—at every event. They reintroduced competitive high school and college field games, nursery rhymes (!), and high school cheerleading routines. These were not considered as entry into a more spiritualized activity, but were an exuberant, countercultural introduction of sociability in the Kenyan church world. The fun brought a remarkably powerful sense of group bonding, but it would be a while before those outside of the Mavuno culture could trust this wild redefinition of church; no wonder Mavuno quickly became known as another cult. As the Marathon took shape, Mavunites kept traditional Christian rituals such as baptisms, baby dedications, and weddings with their sacred, covenantal aspects, but there were also opportunities to go to a pub and celebrate the new life with a few drinks and *nyama choma* (goat meat roasted over open charcoal fire), which would have been a proper celebration in traditional Africa. When life groups eventually emerged, leaders were encouraged to allow the spontaneity of relationships to set the normal rhythms of group life.

Every part of the Mavuno Marathon can similarly be traced to some aspect of creative thinking. As learned in the Nairobi Chapel days, thinking creatively was not about a fixed way of doing things; it was about facing new needs in context. In the founding years, rebuilding new community was central. Each subsequent transitional moment in the life of Mavuno has required new ideas to facilitate the flourishing of the community. For instance, when the staff team grew large, they had to design a workable managerial system. They adopted a leadership structure that they came to call the "leadership pipeline."

Leadership as problem solving. The second lesson Muriu taught Muriithi was to see leadership as problem solving. Muriu developed a discipline of waking up at 2:00 a.m. to pray and study for several hours, and then get through most of his paperwork long before dawn, so that by the time his assistants reported to the office, they would be opening numerous emails and (later) text messages sent as early as 4:00 or 5:00 a.m. Muriu came to the conclusion that the logic of his bold faith, confident prayers, and disciplined lifestyle led to an equally bold vision. To go with his big prayers, he had a large placard hanging in his office that read "Do not limit the greatness of your God by the smallness of your vision."

As with much that shaped Muriu's leadership at this point, the need for bold vision was informed by the leadership malaise of the 1990s. One issue was the prevailing attitude toward leadership, that holding a public office was a source of privilege, an opportunity to cruise, exert power over others, and receive the perks of office, such as a good salary, cars, holidays, and international travels. Second, a latent assumption was that solutions to intractable problems could come from the outside. Dependence was far more insidiously expressed in the political leadership that looked to the West for financial aid instead of building local economies and nurturing talent. However, the churches were not in a much better position, largely because they did not know how to train new leaders and were relying on institution-based theological education and ordination to raise new clergy (which limited women). Muriu said that theological school was too expensive and took a good two to four years to produce a theologically astute minister. Yet when these came in as clergy, they would often be out of touch with real needs in the church because they were sheltered in school. He noticed that university students in their early twenties were energetic, freshly expectant, and often open to mentoring. He recruited these as trainees. Ever the indefatigable and creative go-getter, Muriu set standards that stretched the limits of their energies, knowledge, competencies, and more.

The fact that his interns weren't recruited from theological school did not mean they were not theologically or intellectually capable. In time Muriu systematically built a library of books that he expected his interns to read and review through the year. Bill Hybels of Willow Creek became a significant influence on all the trainees over time, as they read *Who You Are When No One Is Looking, Too Busy Not to Pray,* and *Courageous Leadership* during leadership training at Nairobi Chapel and later Mavuno Church. They were also shaped by Stephen Covey's *Seven Habits of Highly Effective People,* Jim Collins's *Good to Great,* and Andy Stanley's *Visioneering, Next Generation Leader,* and *Practices of Ministry,* as well as a stash of the easy-to-read theological writings of the British evangelical statesman John Stott.

With all the leading, learning, and reading, at some point most interns would develop a love-hate relationship with Muriu as they were stretched to their limits. Much of the angst almost always resolved itself by the end of the year when they graduated and went on to become well-known leaders. At any rate, as Muriu puts it, he knew that his rookies, straight out of the university, were diamonds in the rough when he first identified them, and he did what he had to do to sharpen and polish them.

Muriithi admits that as a young man he was difficult to lead, but Muriu was an equally tough boss who did not entertain excuses. He tersely told interns, "Leaders solve problems, period." Yes, the church was a community of faith, and it was also an organization that needed a vision. The practical steps to turning that vision to reality included planning strategically, mobilizing necessary resources, encouraging ownership within the congregation, and staying the course until one got results. The particular solution needed at any one time is up to the trainee, but the rubric of leadership as problem solving was where Muriu expected his interns to start. When Muriu assigned a task, a trainee did not come back to ask for instructions; neither was an excuse permissible. Muriu would say with finality, "There are nine ways to skin a cat." When a job was done, he did not expect a lengthy report; a simple "Done" was enough. In their turn, interns often said that Muriu "threw you in the deep end of the swimming pool, and sinking was not an option!" That was the "iron sharpening iron" that Muriithi needed in order to become a frontline leader of the next decade.

Raising leaders and delegating responsibility. Third, Muriu did not expect individual heroism among his trainees. As he trained others, he also modeled delegating real leadership responsibility and finding success through enlisting others, both men and women. Remember that Muriu was training his leaders at the juncture when a growing body of literature zeroed in on poor leadership across the board. Public figures, mainly politicians, were seen as clueless at worst and incompetent at best, more concerned about enriching themselves, maintaining tenure, handing out favors to tribal affiliations, and then retiring with largesse. Even in the churches, leaders were aging under the illusion that no one else was equally qualified for the job. In theological circles, there was much talk of the need for servant leaders, following the disconnect between numerical growth of the church and the acute shortage of trained leadership. Theologians such as John Stott, Tokunbo Adeyemo, Tite Tienou, and Mensa Otabil who were then considered thought leaders in the theological world urged churches to intentionally prepare leaders whose ethical, moral, and spiritual values could impact the world of politics, government, and business.

Against this background of disillusionment with the leadership and the possibility of a better way, these ideas caught the imagination of the idealistic and highly energetic Muriu. He did not talk about servant leadership or decry the lack of trained ministers. He simply modeled the answer. The theologians mentioned were directing their leadership-training energies toward seminaries and theological colleges such as NEGST, Nairobi International School of Theology, St. Paul's, and Scott. On the other hand, Muriu had a good problem—he needed more hands "to manage the harvest," as he put it. Nairobi Chapel grew from twenty to eighty people within his first year as confirmed pastor. In three years the numbers were up to five hundred. He adopted Jesus' model of mentoring a few disciples and delegating the work to them. This is when he began to recruit fresh graduates as interns. It is now common to train women in church leadership positions, but back then women's roles were usually limited to pastors' wives, children's pastors, or leaders of women's programs. But Muriu had no such qualms. He expected women such as Janet Mutinda, Marcy Karianjahi, Jane Wathome, Cathleen Rotich, Linda Ochola, Jackie Othoro, and others (including this writer) to deliver on expectations per their gifting and training.

At any rate, making a leader out of a university student began with recognizing fresh potential. Muriu would then nurture the four Cs he considered important: character, competence, chemistry, and comprehension. For character, Muriu had uncompromisingly high expectations of moral integrity. He and his wife not only modeled high standards, he also structured office and ministry arrangements to ensure that no trainee was caught in a position of sexual compromise. For chemistry, he expected trainees to work in teams and relate amiably to the congregation. For competence, excellent performance was expected in whatever an intern was assigned. For comprehension, interns were challenged to develop an enlarged vision through reading widely, not just of the mission of God but a broad understanding of the world so they could be effective. Responsibilities would be given according to both gifting and need in the exponentially growing church. When Muriu sensed that a leader was mature, he would create more opportunities or delegate fully. For instance, in 2004 he took a long-overdue sabbatical and left Muriithi and Janet Mutinda to be the senior pastors of the three-thousand-member congregation. This is how in 2005 each trained pastor also had a cohort of other support pastors and volunteers who had been through internship.

While Muriithi's personal biography and disciplined mentoring are significant, there were key moments that helped him come into his own. The capacity to make the right calls in these moments was rooted in increasing his skill set, showing that being a leader is as much a journey of learning in community as it is a job. The first moment was Muriu's invitation to consider a pastoral career, which built on the quiet influence of his mother and father, whom Muriithi often credits as his premier role models. Another turning point was his bittersweet experience of America. He and Carol were students in the second half of the 1990s, a bad time to live as an African in the United States. Decades of inefficient political mismanagement painted a bleak future for Africa, infamously dubbed "the hopeless continent" by *The Economist* in 2000, right about when Muriithi was completing his studies at Fuller. Africa was a byword for war, disease, illiteracy, dictatorship, corruption, economic stagnation, and backwardness. When he came back to Kenya, he desperately wanted to change that narrative.

The third moment was when he took on full responsibility of Nairobi Chapel in 2004, during the time of impasse in the initial relocation. He was only thirty-three years old, and not everyone thought he should lead because, as with many of Muriu's experiments, there was no precedent for it. Nonetheless Muriu trusted Muriithi and Janet Mutinda to co-lead. They thrived and set the stage for the 2005 multiplication. Another important moment was in 2008 when Muriithi led two hundred pastors in a nationwide reconciliation caravan and faced a nation devastated after the disputed election. That experience changed the face of Africa to a youthful continent. What had been a goal to reach the Nairobi middle class became a vision "to plant a culture-defining church in every capital city of Africa" and to help youth transition into mature adults as fearless influencers of the continent. More recently, leading the church to purchase permanent property in the rapidly developing residence of Athi River posed a daunting challenge to raise a quarter of a billion shillings (US$2,500,000) and to move a crowd that was quite happy in South C. He and his staff team pulled off the move, but just when there was much excitement about it, a controversial teen-ministry poster stoked a raging debate that overshadowed the enormous feat. The years since relocation to the new property have tested the mettle of his leadership, staff, and resources, but Muriithi has settled the church, mentored additional church planters, and is working himself out of the job of senior pastor so that younger pastors can take over.

Having explored Muriithi's own formation as a leader, it is now possible to see how the Mavuno Marathon, his tool for leading change, evolved as a leadership strategy. Nairobi Chapel's vision was "Equipping God's people to disciple the nations for Christ." However, Muriu did not develop such a tool as the Marathon, at least not in the 1990s (though he would develop one after the 2005 relocation). On the other hand, the years of training, mentoring, and extensive exposure, allowed Muriithi to reflect on national and regional problems in terms of a crisis of leadership and to speak openly in sermons, writings, and leadership events on the role of the church in resolving the continent's dilemmas. To him the solution would not be to steer the church into political engagement but rather to develop a fully conceived plan of individual and community change and to raise the aspirational and emerging middle class into an army of fearless influencers who can transform society wherever they are gifted, educated, and connected by work and other social obligations.

New Structures of Leadership

The team at the heart of the action was diversely gifted. Initially, Muriithi started out with four colleagues: Linda Ochola as executive pastor, Simon Mbevi as care pastor, Kanji Mbugua as worship director, and Carol Wanjau as educational pastor. Each already had a degree in the liberal arts in law, banking, pharmaceuticals, media, and psychology, as well as theological training. They also had significant histories running independent initiatives. In that first year they recruited several interns, who, following the Nairobi Chapel culture, already had a university degree. In 2008, when the church grew exponentially, Muriithi quickly had to raise a bigger leadership team. By 2010 he had a staff team of nearly one hundred people, most of them under thirty years of age.

Creating a team out of these diversely gifted persons—with limited resources and in the context of trying to understand the urban dynamics of the changed world—turned out to be a hard lesson for everyone. Muriithi was dealing with a highly assertive generation that did not take a pastor's word at face value. Even though they still respected him, they would question and test the limits of the system before acting on assignments. Along with motivating them to learn and lead, Muriithi had to affirm the gifting, training, and passions of each of his pastors, interns, technical staff, and volunteers—a veritable business startup if ever there was one. This led to a staff-organizing structure that came to be known as the "leadership pipeline," which became allied with the Mavuno Marathon as a leadership tool.

First, Muriithi organized his staff into teams for each step of the Marathon. The Marathon is organized as part of the church's annual calendar, with three seasons in a year, three months in a season, and a one-month break between each season. The experiences of the various curricula form a comprehensive discipleship tool. In the long run, when the Marathon runs as a cycle, it produces a movement culture, which then creates "culture defining churches." The steps clarify the essential roles of differently gifted pastors and volunteers and redistributes them throughout the process. Pastors who are gifted in evangelism, for instance, are placed at the entry levels. Teaching pastors are assigned to the connect level. Shepherding pastors are assigned to life groups, while social justice–oriented pastors serve at the compelled stage. This also makes decision making easy because all the important ministries of the church find a place without diverting the energy of the central leadership, while less visible aspects also receive attention at the relevant stage of the Marathon. This arrangement also allows the Marathon to be a leadership-development strategy for staff and a large number of volunteers.

Muriithi then placed supervisors over each level of the Marathon. The entry point to the staff team is the internship, which is now formalized through human resources (HR) systems thinking. HR-based recruitment to internship employs a rigorous selection process designed to ensure that anyone that joins staff has a vibrant relationship with God, a clear and genuine sense of call to ministry, and a university degree, though not necessarily a theological one. Like Muriu, Muriithi believes that interns coming out of undergraduate universities are flexible and willing to learn, which is necessary because joining Mavuno staff is a steep learning curve. At the internship level, the primary assignment is to learn how to lead and manage oneself, focusing on basics of time, relationships, personal values, administrative tasks, and spiritual disciplines. After interns complete a year, some move to other professions but stay dynamically connected to Mavuno's ministries. Some stay as pastoral trainees, where they are expected to continue leading themselves and others by mobilizing volunteer teams, designing and delegating meaningful tasks, and facilitating team problem solving. The two-year pastoral training is usually a time of confirmation for long-term pastoral work, including planting new congregations. After the two years, some will enter the next level as team managers and senior management staff, who lead the bodies that make decisions about the daily, weekly, and annual calendar. Next is the executive level, which gives overall strategic direction to the church.

The term "leadership pipeline," a concept developed by management coaches Ram Charan, Stephen Drotter, and James Noel, presupposes that a natural hierarchy exists in most organizations, including churches. For an organization to harness talents for its long-term vision, it should enable its staff to grow through what is pictured as a series of passages through a pipeline. Each step allows staff to gain new skills, from managing self, to managing others, to managing managers, to functional managers, to business managers, to group managers, and finally to CEOs. Each passage requires that staff acquire new skills while retaining mastery of earlier steps. The challenge for organizations is to ensure that people in leadership positions are assigned to the level suitable to their skills, that they are developing new capabilities for new responsibilities, and that they have the right values for that point of responsibility.[3]

Mavuno's leadership structure evolved alongside the Mavuno Marathon long before the concept of a pipeline was adopted. Naming it the leadership pipeline allowed the human resources office to professionalize the growing complexity of an organization that now has more than one hundred people on staff, so as to balance official procedure with the organic growth occurring at all levels of the Marathon loop. When the church was less complex, Muriithi and his lead pastors would easily talk over issues after a prayer meeting and a cup of tea. Now each stage of the leadership pipeline outlines expectations and required trainings. The staff, right up to the executive pastors' team, has seasonal classes for every stage of the pipeline. They have quarterly and annual evaluations corresponding to their levels of involvement, to determine extra coaching, reassignment, and staff transitions out of the team. The pipeline allows staff transitions to be worked out without fallout and creates room for new trainees. For instance, Simon Mbevi was one of the founders of Mavuno and was much loved as a care pastor. In 2008 he held a significant responsibility mobilizing the reconciliation within the nation after the postelection violence. By 2009 he knew that his gifting included mobilizing

---

[3]Ram Charan, Stephen Drotter, and James Noel, *The Leadership Pipeline: How to Build the Leadership Powered Company* (San Francisco: Jossey-Bass, 2010).

beyond the Mavuno congregation. He resigned and founded Transform Kenya (see more in chapter five), which became a successful frontline ministry. He remains Muriithi's close friend and is one of Mavuno's preaching pastors, but he is no longer on the staff payroll. Similarly, Kanji Mbugua was the founding worship pastor. He too wanted to expand his skills into business, and after training a group of volunteers to run the worship department, he resigned to start a media agency that supports creative artists, many of whom are from Mavuno. After several years, Cynthia Otieno, who was running the children's department, felt her passion was to coach working mothers, couples, and marriages. She left to start an independent initiative called LaMead Network, but she still serves Mavuno as a high-capacity volunteer. Sophie Mbevi left the staff to start a private school, but like the others she has remained a dedicated volunteer in the marriage ministries.

LEARNING FROM THE SCHOOL OF HARD KNOCKS

Public conflict. While Mavuno is now seen as a very successful church, Muriithi points out that each year it has had intense growing pains, which are in part what have shaped the Marathon. For instance, at the sports club they courted sharp Christian controversy because of unconventional efforts to engage millennials in nightclubs, introducing Afro-soul music as part of Sunday worship, and rewriting Christian lyrics to raunchy hit pop songs, which they called "take backs." Subculture Christians flat out disavowed Mavuno. It was not uncommon for clergy to disparagingly call Mavuno a church of the hippie and New Age, whose gospel is not to be taken too seriously, and call for the young to find themselves and then move to better churches. "Your business is with the trader in the market," says an African proverb. "Let the noise of the market crowd alone." The criticism compelled Muriithi's team to clarify their mission. They concluded that they were going where other churches were not willing to go and, following Paul in Romans 11:13, referred to themselves as "apostles to the Gentiles," though in time this terminology became unwieldy. Their business was to reach the postcollege urbanites, to help them turn their lives around. The "ordinary" were a potentially influential and culture-shaping demographic. This is how they came to frame their mission as "turning ordinary people into fearless influencers of society."

One case of a direct conflict still crops up in public discourse about Mavuno. In February 2014, Mavuno's teen ministry (Teens Konnect) designed a publicity poster showing a young couple in cozy comfort with each other. The poster, titled "Blurred Lines," was intended to advertise Teens Konnect's month-long sermon series addressing what Mavuno perceived as an escalating crisis of teenage sexuality in Nairobi. The sermon titles were to be as provocative as the picture, drawn from hit pop songs that are laced with sexual innuendo, such as "You Can Gerrit," "Friends with a Monster," and "Fifty Shades of Grey."

A media house caught a whiff of the poster and made headlines by labelling it "Porn Poster" on evening primetime news. Immediately, Mavuno was all over the public domain, as incensed debate raged and trended for an entire week on social media, television, and radio talk shows. Everybody weighed in on how low the church had sunk. On the one hand were those who strongly condemned Mavuno. Most people that identified as Christians posted angry comments, critical of Mavuno in no uncertain terms. On the opposite side of the debate, social icons thought the poster was quite tame. Leading media personalities such as Caroline Mutoko, Njoki Chege, and Maina Kageni, whose talk shows are otherwise notorious for pushing boundaries on social conversations, were surprisingly supportive of what Mavuno Church was trying to do—to raise the antennae on the new wave of sexual liberties brought by the mobile and internet revolution. The media gurus argued that the Mavuno church poster barely scratched the surface of the problem of a tech-savvy society without checks and balances. The mobile phone technology had compromised all previous limits of innocence, but before this poster the debate had hardly been brought out in the open. Those condemning the poster as "pornographic" were, in the words of Caroline Mutoko, hypocrites with smartphones.

As a result, Muriithi was invited to several talk shows where he had a chance to publicize Mavuno's vision of reaching young people. And although this was a controversy with strong negative undertones that affected the big relocation, it highlighted Mavuno Church as a different kind of player in Kenya's ecclesial scene, to which it was impossible to attach the old labels of conservativism or liberalism. For instance, in the heat of the TV talk shows, media houses invited well-respected leaders from older churches and their umbrella organizations, such as the National Council of Churches, which are known to be rather traditional. As talk-show hosts are wont to do, they skewed the questions and the pace of the debates so that these respected leaders would condemn Mavuno as too liberal. Instead, many affirmed that Mavuno was known to do radical things that were effective in reaching young people who were missing in the older churches.

Spiritual warfare, prayer, and staff care. The two years spent breaking into the hard ground of South C compelled the staff team to pray intensely. Their avant-garde location at the sports club was poorly accessible because of a stretch of earthen track road. In the dry season, dust ruined the beautiful African outfits of the women. When it rained, cars got stuck in the mud. The club itself was an entertainment spot. The Mavuno team would report by 5:00 a.m. on Sunday mornings to turn the place inside out, to literally wash off alcohol and garbage, set up chairs and worship equipment, and then spend several hours in cleansing prayer before worship. On weekdays the staff rented an apartment in the vicinity where they could work and store their equipment. It was also during that difficult season that Simon Mbevi, one of the pastors, wrote the prayer-focused curriculum Ombi for the staff team, which eventually grew into a blueprint for one of the Marathon classes. Volunteers also started other prayer-focused activities, including a Wednesday-morning men's prayer gathering from 5:00 to 7:00 a.m., which they called Gideon's Torch.

It was during this learning season that staff care became an important aspect of leadership development. Muriithi, a natural go-getter, tended to focus more on risk-taking activities to reach millennials. But the women on the leadership team, especially Linda Ochola and Carol Wanjau, steered him toward nurturing the staff team first. Through a variety of weekly, seasonal, and annual staff-care activities, they transformed the staff into a sort of family. To date, the staff take Mondays off as their sabbath day, then they hold staff church on Tuesday mornings, in which they spend two hours in worship, prayer, and various activities of pastoral care. As part of keeping an energized and aligned team they have a fun offsite annual staff retreat, as well as several smaller recreational retreats. The large staff team may work together on the Marathon, but, by and large, operations are decentralized under department heads.

Muriithi says it has made a big difference to his leadership to pay attention not only to the skills and gifts, but the "sixth sense" of leaders with different personalities, especially the women pastors. These differences are part of why the leadership pipeline took shape to address the formal administrative features of running the church, while the team could still care for one another as a family and maintain a pastoral posture toward their large cohort of volunteers. Professionally skilled staff run the payroll, facilities, human resources, and other supervisory affairs. They leave Muriithi out of the center of managerial problem solving so that he can mentor his pastors, trainees, and volunteers from a relational standpoint. Although he is quite close to them in age, he affectionately calls the young pastors his "sons and daughters," and many extend the same familial kinship toward him and his wife. For most congregants, he has become a father figure because he has walked with them along a transformational mile, out of a dysfunctional lifestyle to a place where they are fearlessly pursuing their purpose. In the next chapter, we will see the impact of this message and leadership in transformed lives.

5

Mavuno Church's Impact

A Fearless Influence on Society

If you ask Muriithi Wanjau what sets Mavuno Church apart, he will not name the Mavuno Marathon, the innovative leadership pipeline, or the visibility in socially controversial issues. He will talk about that first experimental class with a bunch of unruly millennials. Over the years, Muriithi has watched the progressive transformation of that core group into fearless influencers having remarkable impact as witnesses to the gospel. Every changed person represents a better friend, a wholesome marriage, a company that is doing ethical business, a neighborhood where residents watch out for the community, and so on. Muriithi will point to testimonies where people talk about how God has turned them into fearless influencers. The common refrain is "I'm not what I'd like to be, but I'm sure not what I used to be!" This chapter shows how the pieces fit together and then offers a few of the stories that feature at Mavuno events.

Pivotal Perspective: Evangelical Revitalization

Andrew Walls tells a story of how, as a well-trained church historian with a pedigree from universities in the United Kingdom, he was serving as a missionary in West Africa. Part of his role included teaching second-century church history to African students, which he framed in terms of the history of the church in the West. One day it dawned on him that he was living in the midst of a Christianity that resembled that of the second-century church. The church was taking shape among cultures that were coming to terms with a first-time encounter between the Christian religion, traditional religions, and other cultural realities. In his words, he stopped pontificating and started observing. His observations have led to our expanded understanding of the shift of Christianity from the Global North to its making a homeland across the Global South.

Mark Shaw is a historian raised and educated in the Reformed Christian tradition. In the 1980s, he and his wife, Lois, and their two children relocated to Kenya as missionaries and settled to teach church history in several theological colleges. Like Andrew Walls before him, Shaw observed the fervent indigenous churches of rural and low-income urban Africa. He looked at the literature from a century of fervent indigenous Christianities across Africa, Latin America, and Asia.[1] Whereas most individual congregations were small, the sum of the movements they birthed displayed certain trajectories of beginnings, growth, and predictable results. The histories of these movements have been documented by older and younger Africanist scholars across the spectrum, such as David Barrett, Ogbu Kalu, Allan Anderson, and Asamoah Gyadu.[2] Interestingly, many of these movements also grew into what would be called megachurches today, but at the time there wasn't much interest in this phenomenon. Gyadu makes a strong case that the older thread of indigenous continuity in this reformation has now evolved into the contemporary, well-known megachurches in Africa, particularly in Nigeria. He believes the current megachurches are growing because they are excelling in engaging the three interrelated publics of the modern African moral universe: the village that remains connected to the primal imagination of the African past, the emergent urban public that is characteristic of a modernizing world, and the Western globalizing public that is drawing Africans into the wider circle of the world. These churches are reaching the new African person because of their ability to associate with each of these populations, while not antagonizing the others.[3]

---

[1] See especially the introductory chapter of Mark Shaw, *Global Awakening: How 20th-Century Revivals Triggered a Christian Revolution* (Downers Grove, IL: IVP Academic, 2010).

[2] See especially Ogbu Kalu, *African Pentecostalism: An Introduction* (New York: Oxford University Press, 2008); Allan Anderson, *African Reformation: African Initiated Christianity in the 20th Century* (Trenton, NJ: Africa World Press, 2001); J. Kwabena Asamoah-Gyadu, *Contemporary Pentecostal Christianity: Interpretations from an African Context* (Eugene, OR: Wipf & Stock, 2013).

[3] J. Kwabena Asamoah-Gyadu, "Pentecostalism in Africa," in *African Theology on the Way: Current Conversations*, ed. Diane B. Stinton, SPCK International Study Guide 46 (London: SPCK, 2010), 59.

Be that as it may, what Shaw found out was that usually a movement began in socially volatile, changing worlds where there is loss of faith in the legitimacy of established institutions and a general crisis of belief in the religious sphere. The transforming idea would first crystallize in the experience of a prophetic leader who is drawn into the heart of the crisis via personal predicament. Once such a leader internalized the grievances of his time in himself, he would articulate the crisis to a larger sphere. In time a cohort of followers resonated not only with his prophetic premonitions, but also his vision of revitalizing society through a message rooted into the gospel. But this leader had to translate that message into terms that would resonate with current concerns. When he did, he attracted a following, along with some opposition. The followers then grew into communities and congregations which over a generation spread as large movements in vast regions. Scholars have variously referred to the movements as African Indigenous Churches (AICs), Pentecostal and charismatic movements, and independent churches.

Shaw proposes that nearly all such revival movements, even the African indigenous ones, retrace their roots to eighteenth-century evangelical Christianity through the missionary movement, and therefore can be analyzed in the tradition of the evangelical revivals. In new times and new cultural settings, these movements arise as "charismatic people movements that transform their cultural world by translating Christian truth and transferring the power of the gospel to new generations." Shaw calls the movements that have spanned several generations and large geographic regions "global revivals" or "global awakenings."[4] Arguably, most of these movements are spiritual *revivals*, yet the pattern he shows through the case studies is that most only go part of the way as *revitalizing* influences in the wider world. The emphases they place on culture, church tradition, and various aspects of the New Testament determine how far their kind of Christianity becomes a revitalizing influence in contemporary society. These patterns are all possible to trace, for instance, in AIC Christianities, Pentecostal groups, movements such as the East African Revival, and the Catholic Charismatic movement.[5]

---

[4]Shaw, *Global Awakening*, 29.
[5]See Shaw, *Global Awakening*, 203-6.

Shaw argues that if a movement is to bring about a full *evangelical revitalization*, that is, transform individuals, form community, and grow to have widespread influence on society, there is a discernible trajectory. First, the unexpected entry of global forces into local cultures that are otherwise functional is often a trigger for profound social volatility. When dominating forces intrude, they challenge the worldviews of the old systems and disturb the continuity, order, and predictability of functional social institutions. Social stress starts to be felt in ordinary life—disobedient youth, alcoholism, relational and marital breakdown, rising crime, poorly functioning institutions, and so on. As the old and tested ways of doing things—the maps of reality—fail to solve problems emerging with the new influences, many keep trying to fix the broken maps with new ideas. Older and conservative leaders—old light fundamentalists—complain that the young have left their traditions and attempt call people back to them, which often produces cultural nativistic movements, such as Mungiki. Religious leaders try to lead people back to stricter religious practices. Market, civic, and political leaders cling tightly to bureaucratic power structures while creating scapegoats of the opposition. Over time, deep cultural trauma debilitates the entire society, and because all the recommendations for societal renewal are trying to fix old, broken maps, there is only increasing fragmentation. Shaw refers to this as the *relativization* of local cultures.

For a movement with a revitalizing influence of an evangelical nature to emerge out of a fragmented society, a "new light leader" (a charismatic individual or a prophetic figure) from the margins presents the gospel in a way that shows marginalized people the way forward. Such a leader connects the teachings of Jesus and New Testament Christianity with the hopes of an alienated generation. The message acts as a turning point that begins to shift the individual through a conversion experience, to deeper commitment in relationship with God, to recovery of identity and belonging with the new community, and beyond to extending this message to the broader world as part of God's mission. There may be conflict and spiritual warfare while trying to shift from the old maps of reality into the new light. There are also new wineskins, that is leadership structures that develop with these shifts, because the old structures, the old wineskins, cannot contain the new message. When a movement successfully develops through these stages, it moves to the power stage. The power stage is when social capital is built among new converts, and they become not only joyful Christians but responsible family members, productive employees, and good citizens. The cumulative impact of the group starts to be felt in the socially dysfunctional world as it brings new light to the old, broken order.

In effect, this has been the story of Mavuno Church.

The preceding narrative has told how prolonged volatility kept building up through generations in the Kenyan situation. Global forces—beginning with colonialism, followed by the postcolonial malaise, and finally technology-driven cultural globalization—led to a forceful relativizing impact on the world of urban millennials in the late 1990s and early 2000s. Part of this demographic was awakened to the message of the gospel at Nairobi Chapel through Oscar Muriu, who led a spiritual revival there. A socially revitalizing awakening (not just a revival) of the millennials as a generation would require a message that helped to connect their aspirations to the gospel, that is, to the discovery of purpose through recovery of relationship with God and community. The awakened millennial demographic would grow into a movement through leadership and structures that took shape around this renewed sense of purpose and relationships.

In Mavuno, as a ten-year-old congregation, all this is still evolving, but the outline is already strong. The transforming power of the new paradigm is initially felt at the individual level. Personal liberation affirms that contrary to the previous sense of rootlessness, individuals are much-loved sons and daughters of God. Contrary to the helplessness in the face of overwhelming odds, God has a plan for their lives, achieved with the support of their newfound community and rooted in God's greater purposes. As individuals grow into a community, the change that has come over them turns into witness, first to friends and family, then to other spheres of influence. This witness also includes the reassertion of local cultural products and local identity. Other members attend to issues of justice in the community by starting frontline initiatives. According to Shaw, if this trajectory endures in the long term, large-scale social and political change may grow out of the movement. The fullest expression of an evangelical revitalization movement comes with systemic change, whereby, in addition to the spiritually revived nation or regions, political, economic, and social systems are vividly changed by ongoing application of gospel values and practices into the wider society. *Glocalization* is also part of missional influence, where the local and the global evangelicals join the global highway to take their movement to regional and international levels, creating two-way, global-cultural traffic. This is a response to the global conditions that first relativized local cultures; movements want to spread their influence.[6]

The impact of an evangelical revitalization movement becomes obvious in historical hindsight after the movement has been active over a longer period of time. So far, as we will see in the stories below, the foregoing narrative fits the bill of what is taking place at Mavuno Church. Recall in parts of chapters one and two, I talked about the sense of homelessness, feeling out of sync and thus experiencing a loss of identity. At Mavuno, the person who has experienced transformation reclaims their personal identity, as the following story will show.

RECOVERING PERSONAL IDENTITY:
UNDER NEW MANAGEMENT

Many Christians, when they have experienced the saving power of the gospel, will sing the words of John Newton's "Amazing Grace":

> I once was lost, but now am found,
> > Was blind, but now I see.

In Mavuno testimonies, a common refrain has become "My life is under new management." This is an expression of personal liberation, where an individual has a sense of radical differentiation from the life they lived before their experience at Mavuno Church and their life after conversion in the community. Biographical testimonials are a common feature of Mavuno Church services, events, and blogs. Chero is one such person. In her early twenties, she got married while living in America, but the marriage quickly turned sour through physical abuse. Within a short while, the marriage was annulled. To dull her confusion, Chero turned to partying wildly. She says that she would basically ride in every fast lane of personal indulgence to get any high that would numb the pain of the abuse she had experienced, which only led her deeper into the brokenness.

---

[6]Shaw, *Global Awakening*, 28, 202.

She returned to Kenya as a disillusioned young woman and continued to spiral downward.

Watching the path of self-destruction that she was taking, one of Chero's friends dragged the rather reluctant young woman to Mavuno and enrolled her in a Mizizi class. Chero did not believe that church could offer her anything relevant to her hopes as a young woman or cure the pain of her past. Yet, out of respect for her friend, she attended the class. From the first day, she dived into the heated discussions, initially to disprove anything positive about God or church. The Mizizi facilitator allowed her to express her strongly scandalous views and her doubts. There were others like her, as wrecked and skeptical and rambunctious. Eventually the acceptance and honest atmosphere in the class led them to talk about the real shadows behind their objections to God and faith. They began to let go of their caricatures and explored Bible stories to find what God's image really was. Chero came to the realization that she did not have to be defined by a broken past. A good future with Christ at the center was possible. Before the ten-week course ended, she let go of objections and opened to a powerful experience of forgiveness in a flood of tears. She accepted a new identity as a much-loved child of God. In her own words, considering what she had been through, the experience was powerfully liberating, affirming, and filled with the possibility of a bright future. Her lifestyle would take a little while longer to turn around, but her Mizizi group allowed her to take it one step at a time. One of the first things she did was to drag her boyfriend to the next Mizizi class. He too began a similar journey and eventually they decided to formalize their relationship through marriage. They took the NDOA class and exchanged wedding vows. Chero, a gifted thespian with a bubbly personality, went on to become a high-capacity volunteer, hosting Sunday services and acting and doing spoken word in them. In 2011 she enrolled in Mavuno's internship, where she explored how she could use her life as a testimony to others now in her former situation. After her internship, she took a job with a leading media house where she sees herself as a witness to young women. She also continues to serve in the Mavuno services department as a host, artist, and media consultant.

This is the story of thousands that have come through Mavuno. After Chero found that the Mavuno community was a place with enough grace to welcome her skepticism, she learned to trust church leadership and listen to their teaching until she came to a saving relationship with Christ. She found new community that helped her life to stabilize.

Stories like hers are publicly available on the Mavuno website and blogs. The details differ—from miraculous or gradual transformation out of alcoholic habits, uninhibited clubbing lifestyles, involvement in crime, abdicating family responsibilities, personality-related conflicts, failing marriages—but the trajectory often begins when a reluctant individual is introduced to Mavuno by a friend whose life has been turned around. Some will come intermittently and sit back aloofly for months, listening and watching suspiciously before they engage. There are also those who don't come with "colorful" backgrounds but are simply looking for a community that understands them. They also tell how Mavuno Church awakens their love for God and helps to frame their perception of contemporary issues. Gradually, people come to faith in God and to trust Mavuno as a place they can belong.

Chero is frequently heard telling her testimony to get someone else started in the journey of transformation. She says she lived recklessly because, as a hurting person, "I didn't know any better because no one had shown me what is better," but "Thank God, Mercy said no!" and led her to Mavuno where she has found a home, built a good marriage, made new Christian friends, and discovered a passionate purpose. Such stories of what life was like before Mavuno, how Mavuno transformed someone, and what life is like at the present are regularly shared in Mavuno services, classes, retreats, mission trips, trainings, and leaders' days.

Chero has discovered, however, as many others have, that the journey from the old reality where Christ is marginal to a new reality is not accomplished in the few steps of plugging into church or accepting Christ. The actual lifestyle involves learning, growing, pushing back against the darkness, and overcoming life's frustrations inside and outside the church. Perhaps this is one of the hardest things for those who first come to faith, even at Mavuno. The overwhelming sense of acceptance and the encouraging testimonies make it seem easy to be a Christian. Over time that excitement dies down as routine settles in, which is why there is a significant backdoor. Even those in the closest circle of the church activities may leave, leaders not excluded. Some go to other churches because after a while they say Mavuno is not teaching a "deep word." Those who stay, however, recognize the real work of developing Christlike character is connected to participating in the Mavuno Marathon in its totality, not merely attending Sunday services, going to a single class, or making friends. It is the journey.

Mavuno pastors have come to recognize these initial "spiritual highs" and know these are inadequate to sustain faith over the long term. Therefore, there is a constant emphasis on belonging to a life group, building relationships through family ministries, and serving in the community, as well as sermons that help connect faith to life in the wider society. Many do proceed through the five stages of the Marathon. Some, like Chero, make a personal impact on friends, family, and their work places. Then there is another category of people who, once they find their place in Mavuno, their faith goes on steroids and their actions reach far beyond personal influence, as the following stories show.

RECLAIMING CULTURAL IDENTITY: CLEANING THE AIRWAVES

As we saw earlier, following the sweeping influx of global trends, the local cultural world always takes a hit. At such times of relativization of local identities, people begin to feel like strangers in their own country. Following the awakening of a new generation, new leaders help their followers to rediscover, reevaluate, and embrace the local cultures—customs, values, artifacts—and integrate them with the invading foreign cultures, creating a whole new set of cultural products.

Mavuno Church triggered the awakening of constructive creativity in the entire entertainment industry, reclaiming the sphere from the wilderness of global-cultural products. Just as with the rewriting of basic discipleship, none of this took place through theological pontificating. It was all trial and error, for which Mavuno took plenty of flak. As pointed out in chapter two, the influx of global media in the 1990s introduced stale Western content, including music, movies, and television productions. Each technological upgrade—television channels, the internet, mobile phones, smartphones with multiple capacities of communication, advertising, and social media—brought further shockwaves of alienating content. Music, especially the sexually explicit variety broadcast by numerous radio stations, had become the epitome of self-expression for urban youth. When Muriithi and his team faced up to the fact that "Mike" and "Makena" would not be reached through street and soapbox evangelism, they also realized that Mavuno had to find bridges to culture, art, and especially music.

To bridge this cultural communication gap, they established a social-media presence. Today the use of social media is widespread, so advertising church events through Facebook, Twitter, and Instagram does not seem like a big deal. But between 2005 and 2010, when these platforms were just hitting the market, Mavuno was pushing conventional boundaries of religious experience. Even more vital was for them to deal with the runaway musical arena. In the Christian scene, so-called contemporary Christian music (CCM), consisting mostly of white artists and genres, had become popularized by a well-loved, subcultural, foreign-content Christian radio station called Radio316. By now the Hosanna! Integrity and Maranatha labels from the Nairobi Chapel days had become passé, even among urban Christians. New voices, including Darlene Zschech, Don Moen, Michael W. Smith, Chris Tomlin, Jars of Clay, and Hillsong United, were played on Radio316. In another new move, Mavuno's creative team adopted and popularized the music of Afro-American gospel singers. At the time the music of African American artists did not get much airplay on Radio316. Mavuno brought in the African Americans to its own audience as a better bridge to African urban youth. Afro-American gospel music is rooted in an experiential expression of faith, and thus is more emotive, energetic, and community oriented than the mellow, vertically focused white music.

One signature musician Mavuno adopted in worship was Kirk Franklin. Franklin had been singing since the early 1990s with the Nu Nation gospel band. In the late 1990s his R & B funk song "Stomp" struck a mutinous note for that era, even in America. He began the song with these spoken words:

For those of you that think gospel music has gone too far . . .
Well I got news for you, you ain't heard nothin' yet,
and if you don't know, now you know. Glory Glory!

In 1990s America, dominated as it was by the secular urban contemporary genres of hip-hop, R & B, and soul, Kirk Franklin's music created a bridge between African American Christians with traditional choirs and performance-based R & B music. Franklin's style proved to be popular with both Christian and non-Christian audiences, and many others have followed in his footsteps. At Mavuno, Franklin's music, along with that of other African American gospel singers such as Israel Houghton, Karen Sheard, Mary Mary, and Donnie McClurkin replaced the typical CCM options. Franklin's "Imagine Me," for instance, became a worship staple at Mavuno, as it expressed well what Mavunites like Chero were experiencing as they went through the Mizizi class:

Imagine me
Loving what I see when the mirror looks at me 'cause I . . .
I imagine me, in a place of no insecurities
And I'm finally happy 'cause
I imagine me
Letting go of all of the ones who hurt me
'Cause they never did deserve me
Can you imagine me?
Saying no to thoughts that try to control me
Remembering all you told me
Lord, can you imagine me?
Over what my mama said, and healed from what my daddy did
And I wanna live and not read that page again
Imagine me, being free, trusting you totally, finally I can
Imagine me
I admit it was hard to see, you being in love with someone like me
But finally I can
Imagine me

To complement the songs of the African American artists, the worship team wrote music, which was popularized by the Mavuno Worship Project. One of the hits from that project was "I Am Under the Rock," complete with footwork, power moves, and hand swipes borrowed from the gym. But Mavuno's craziest approach was to "take back" songs in church. "Take-backs" were common secular songs for which the team would write new Christian lyrics and sing as part of worship. This caused a lot of controversy among Nairobi churches, but the Mavunites who used to frequent the clubs loved the take-backs. To support all this musical activity, the folksy Nairobi Chapel choir was replaced by a popular neo-soul band that could play as well in church as in nightclubs.

Kanji Mbugua and MWAPI. The brain behind this musical turnaround at Mavuno Church was Kanji Mbugua, who was Muriithi's friend whom he met during his theological studies in the United States. Mbugua was raised in a middle-class Christian family in Nairobi and had pursued music since he was young. In 1997 he enrolled at Biola University in California to study music and vocal performance, as well as learning audio engineering and the music business from the Musicians Institute in Hollywood and the Dallas Sound Lab. While studying he and some Kenyan childhood friends—Kaima Mwiti, Harry Njuguna, and Christian Mungai—formed the Christian music group Milele, recorded three albums together, and toured the United States and East Africa. Their song "Sanjolama" was a hit in East Africa in the late 1990s. Mbugua returned to Kenya in 2004 and started Kijiji Records.

During their time in the United States this group met Muriithi and he became the group's pastoral mentor. When Muriithi planted Mavuno in 2005, Mbugua joined the team as the worship director. He recruited several budding musicians for Mavuno's worship and creative team. Muriithi and Mbugua mentored these musicians through a Mizizi class, which helped them to mature as Christians and to become a support group for one another as artists. Mavuno weekend services and creative outreach activities affirmed their talent and began to give them a platform to sharpen their skills by leading in worship or providing input into the creative design of the services. Mavuno also gave them a home as artists. As one of them reports, at the time it was radical for a church to welcome entertainers who were not necessarily singing gospel lyrics or performing in churches and let them identify with the church as their performing base. Opening the space to so-called non-Christian musicians and activities was part of the reason Mavuno was viewed as a cult by outsiders, while Mavuno considered itself a countercultural church. The censure notwithstanding, Mavuno showed the young, talented artists that they did not have to sing specifically religious lyrics in order to create wholesome entertainment. They could perform in clubs and at non-Christian events.

Today several of the artists from that initial group of musicians that Mbugua mentored are household names in the Kenyan mainstream entertainment industry. Aaron "Krucial Keys" is the leading jazz artist in East Africa, who performs at jazz festivals and runs a radio program on Capital FM, a secular radio station. Juliani has grown into a household name for music that addresses social and political issues in the low-income areas of Nairobi. His song "Bahasha ya Ocampo" is a sociopolitical critique of the handling of the chief suspects of the postelection violence. It refers to prosecutor Luis Moreno Ocampo of the International Court of Justice in The Hague, who identified and prosecuted six political figures as largely responsible for violence. "Utawala" (leadership), "Exponential Potential," and other creative titles challenge youth to rise up as leaders in the present moment, contrary to Moi's reprimand in the 1990s that they should wait for tomorrow. Juliani's lyrical versatility and creativity is so legendary among the youth that he has been recruited to be a United Nations ambassador to the youth, to challenge them to civic engagement, entrepreneurial creativity, and responsible living. Atemi Oyungu, another from that early era, is said to be the Kenyan "diva" of Afro-fusion. She performs in high-end cultural entertainment settings. She is also a consultant with the Tusker Project Fame, which is about nurturing local talent and producing music suited to Kenyan issues in place of the American hip-hop that is quite removed from African reality. Neema Ntalel, a Cora Award–winning artist, and Dan Aceda (Chizi), who performs in leading clubs, are others that Mbugua and Muriithi mentored together. This small group of artists became the inspiration for other aspiring youth to find their voice and gave birth to a decent entertainment industry that does not necessarily label itself as Christian but is fresh and locally produced and has therefore created a wide range of jobs.

Mbugua's creative team branded this initiative of mentoring young musicians and helping them carry that influence into the wider society as Music with a Positive Influence (MWAPI). Mbugua, along with his wife, Mwendie, incorporated this initiative into their business, Kijiji Media. Through MWAPI, Kijiji meets entertainment needs created by popular culture. By developing artists, shaping their gifts, and making quality productions, they inspire the youth to pursue productive lives that can transform communities.

Mavuno also nurtured another crop of creative artists—writers, actors, poets, and comedians, who alongside the musicians translated Christmas and Easter narratives into Kenyan drama. Each year the teams would showcase a fresh version of these Bible stories to thousands in several shows hosted at the drive-in dome over a holiday weekend. Actors such as Yafesi Musoke, Chero, Jazz Mistri, Sarah Rimbui, and Steve Katingima are now household names involved in the aesthetic production of Kenyan pop media that reflects a mellowing responsiveness to Africanness among the youth. That turn is still happening, as the older, trashy influences continue to sweep the local scene and government regulations are yet to catch up with local talent, but at least there are Kenyan options of locally produced drama such as *Mother-in-Law, Housewives of Kawangware, Tahidi High*, bridal shows, and women's talk shows. While the local media producers of these shows are not affiliated with Mavuno, the initial and crucial local-cultural awareness and embrace, including increased viewership and jobs created out of these programs, were triggered by the cultural turn enabled by Mavuno artists. Likewise, there are other types of creatives, including African fashion and jewelry designers such as Ann Nzilani and Mancini Migwi who trace their creative inspiration to Mavuno. Professionally trained photographer Mwangi Kirubi honed his photography skills at Mavuno events, and now Clicking with a Purpose exists to "rebrand Africa one click at a time." Kirubi is leading some brilliant photographers to showcase the beauty of the exotic as well as the commonplace in Kenyan and African life, thereby "unscrambling Africa."[7]

A-Star and culture-shaping icons (CSIs). Some artists started specific initiatives to have an even greater impact on art, culture, and media. Evangelical revitalization involves the recovery of identity and local converts' sense of purpose beyond their own dream to a bigger dream. New converts

---

[7]See Mwangi Kirubi's website and blog, *Clicking with Purpose*, http://mwarv.click.co.ke/.

not only experience personal life change, they may make a shift from some achievable human goal to a bold vision of God at work through them. This shift in purpose includes a change in values and behavior from vanity, which says, "We can do anything through money or technology or education," or fatalism, which says "We are powerless in the face of strong challenges such as economic disempowerment," to a certainty that "We can do all things through Christ who strengthens us." This is the story of Richard Njau, commonly known by his stage name, A-Star.

Raised as a privileged, middle-class kid, he attended the best schools in Kenya and furthered his education in England and South Africa. As he readily admits, he was one of the youth who had fully embraced Western cultural imports. Because he is a gifted lyricist, he attracted a wide fan base, "groupies," as he calls them. He aspired to be a famous hip-hop, "gangsta" artist. But alongside his musical artistry he lived the characteristic, fast-paced rebellious life throughout his school years and beyond, mimicking the American gangsta lifestyle. A-Star was trying to find balance between living his rebel lifestyle and accomplishing his dream of becoming a big-time musician when Mbugua recruited him to the Mavuno creative team. By that time A-Star was familiar with the mess that goes with the secular hip-hop industry, not only the lyrical cussing but also the problems of alcohol, drugs, and nightclub licentiousness. In an interview during a Mavuno service, he said that he had seen it all and tried it all.

A-Star's sense of purpose shifted when he got saved through Mizizi and the mentoring group, and he began to detest the problems associated with the hip-hop industry. Nevertheless, he still loved the hip-hop genre. Contributing to Mavuno's creative efforts under Mbugua's mentoring led A-Star to an affirmation of his gifting in music and the realization that he did not have to give it up but could channel his talents and passion toward a God-honoring purpose. Inspired, he discovered a call to change the entertainment industry. His love for hip-hop resonated with many other young people who would appreciate clean content, so he decided he would produce hip-hop content whose message is uplifting, educational, and motivating, to counter the vulgar and derogatory content of other expressions of hip-hop. A-Star began an initiative called Cleaning the Airwaves (CTA), whose purpose is to develop culture-shaping icons (CSIs) who create, distribute, and promote MWAPI—family-friendly media content that promotes healthy attitudes toward relationships, sex, work, life, and faith.

Although A-Star's faith formation and discovery of purpose was initially not a smooth ride, he continues to be a high-capacity volunteer at Mavuno as he runs his CTA initiative. He has grown to become a talent manager and producer for budding artists and leading cultural icons. He was also recruited by Google's African office to develop content and host a web platform that has urbane African content that gets up to a million hits every month. A-Star believes he is transforming the morals of young people through the site.

Kevin Mulei and the Groove Awards. We have seen that one may turn personal liberation and faith into good professional work and family ethics, as Chero did. One may also acquire an enlarged sense of purpose, as A-Star did, or find a wonderful community and create a niche business or ministry like Mwangi Kirubi. But it is another thing altogether to follow a dream that becomes a catalyst for major societal reform in a crucial sector of society, which what Kevin Mulei did.

Mulei moved from his rural home in Ukambani to Nairobi as a teenager. In his early twenties, he interacted with older gospel musicians in the city and realized that although they worked hard to create music, they received little appreciation and virtually no income. Churches and schools would invite them to perform, but because the church had become accustomed to "freebie culture" (receiving all kinds of free gifts from Christian organizations abroad), even the musical services of local artists were presumed to be free, without much thought given to the costs of creating a music career. Musicians could hardly make ends meet because whatever they managed to produce was pirated in the black market. Therefore, even with evidence of latent talent, throughout the nineties and the early years of the millennium, the local gospel-music industry was completely lethargic. It is no wonder that rebellious secular music had such a hypnotic effect on the minds of young people. In urban settings, apart from certain oft-repeated choruses, new gospel music was not a feature in most churches, and Radio316 mostly propagated white music. Local Christian musicians fizzled out after a few otherwise popular productions.

In 2004 Mulei, an unemployed twenty-three-year-old, organized what he called JC Groove, a small event at a restaurant in the city center to popularize gospel music. It was a start, but it did not achieve much success. The next year he launched a bigger event in a more popular venue, but it left him with staggering debt. Discouraged, Mulei took a break from the industry and nearly forgot about it. The turning point in his vision came in 2007, while he was attending Mavuno. He had taken the Mizizi class and joined a life group. Still passionate about the welfare of gospel musicians and feeling frustrated about his inability to help them, he shared his dream with his life group. Around that time Muriithi was preaching a sermon series about ordinary people growing into fearless influencers of society. Muriithi had highlighted Kenyan arts and media as one of those sectors of society badly in need of radical transformation because it is the gateway to popular culture. Mulei explained his passion to transform this sector by raising the standards of the gospel-music industry, thus making music available to a wider Kenyan audience, empowering musicians, and offering content for those radio and TV stations that wanted clean, local talent. This would simultaneously popularize gospel music as an evangelistic tool among the youth. His dilemma was that he did not have sufficient resources or ideas of how to make this dream come true.

Mulei's life group took up the challenge of organizing a gospel talent event in 2008. They mobilized musicians to write and produce, recruited Kenyan companies as sponsors, advertised, and oversaw public voting procedures via text messaging. Finally, after nearly a year of planning, they held a ticketed, sold-out gala at the Tsavo Ballroom in the Kenyatta International Conference Center (the largest international conference center in Nairobi). The event, called the Groove Awards, turned out to be an exceptional showcase of gospel-music talent.

This event was the turning point for the gospel-music industry in Kenya. The Groove Awards are now held annually. Every year the "Groove committee" invites musicians to submit high-quality gospel music espousing strong Christian values that has been produced and released to the public within the year. Since it's an annual event, the industry is always fresh and active with new talent. The competition factor raises the standards of songwriting and production, but the awards gala is designed to celebrate all talent and unite the musicians, so that even those that do not win get public recognition, and their music still reaches the market because it is played before votes are taken. The categories of nomination include a wide array of genres, including music in local languages to celebrate the beauty and diversity of Kenyan communities. On the popular level, this has encouraged appreciation of local cultures in place of the previously divisive deprecation of Kenyan's ethnic differences (even though politicians still try to divide people for political gain). Awards include male and female artists of the year, songwriter of the year, outstanding contributor to the gospel-music industry, ethnic regions, gospel radio show, gospel television, gospel group, radio presenter, album, dance, worship, collabo, and even a life-time-achievement award for older musicians, among many others. The awards evolve every year to create room for as much talent as possible. These selections also encourage other collaborators, such as television and radio stations, to see the youth as a resource.

Once the nominations are made, the Groove panel publicizes the nominees and invites public voting via text and online platforms. The panel then mobilizes companies to sponsor Groove events. Corporations pay for advertising because gospel musicians attract thousands of youth fans to Groove tours that precede the final gala night. Mulei says that the Groove tours in major towns have replaced what used to be called open-air crusades. Young people come for entertainment but also hear the gospel through the music as an effective and immediate medium of encouragement, evangelism, and inspiring faith action that influences positive behavior and promotes good in society. The awards have also helped the musicians to find other opportunities, and because of the creativity required, youth also identify with Christian musicians as role models. According to Mulei, the churches are now reaping the benefits as youth now find it cool to be Christian because their role models are award-winning Christian artists. To see the impact, one only needs to look at the Kenyan music posted on YouTube: all genres of gospel music, regardless of the language, have hundreds of thousands of hits, whereas non-gospel music produced by Kenyan musicians is nowhere near so popular. At the gala night and in subsequent media interviews, winners such as Rose Muhando of Tanzania, Betty Bayo, Jimmy Gait, Gloria Muliro, Juliani, Daddy Owen, and others who have grown to be household names, have told stories of their humble family backgrounds, further modeling to the poorest of the youth that anyone can rise up to their potential.

Mulei's initiative is also vital to making an important case for financing mission initiatives in urban Africa. Previously churches, influenced by a mindset from the West, viewed corporations and media houses through the secular-sacred dichotomy and so wanted little to do with corporations. The Groove Awards brought several hitherto-unrelated partners into a symbiotic rapport: gospel musicians, the corporate business world, media, and churches. The corporation Safaricom Limited, the leading telecommunications company in Kenya (owning more than 65 percent of the mobile industry), is the biggest sponsor of the Groove Awards every year. Large media houses like NTV, KTN, and Citizen have sponsored the event by broadcasting it live on television because they want the audience. Mulei's original problem was that musicians hardly got recognition or pay and therefore found a gospel-music career hard to sustain. Now they receive publicity that sells their music, and corporations hire the musicians for independent ventures that depend on the symbiotic relationship of public relations and sponsorship.

Is this liaison between the corporate world and the gospel industry a sellout to consumer culture? Muriithi repudiates this idea: The church in Africa has to find alternative, legitimate ways of funding mission activities. Unlike the church in the West, the nascent church in Africa is not backed by powerful donors, even when considering token donations toward child sponsorship or handpicked development projects. Most congregations are not able to raise enough tithes and offerings to meet regular ministry needs, let alone support auxiliary industries like the production of gospel music. This corporate symbiotic relationship that Kevin Mulei has harnessed with his Groove Awards is one model of raising funds for gospel activities, which shows that money, success, and the gospel do not have to be antagonistic—if the priorities are kept right by all the players involved. So far the Groove Awards have kept that balance because they are run by a man with a solid faith, who is driven by a sense of purpose and has surrounded himself with others who share his vision and hold him accountable.

What about the quality of the music produced by Groove artists? Does it meet the standards of the gospel? David Kuria, who has been chairman of the Groove Awards committee for consecutive seasons, is also the pastor in charge of communication and strategy at Mavuno Church. Kuria says that all art forms, including music, have a perennial challenge of how to balance the artistic beauty and missional quality of the art itself with the need to be self-sustaining. The entertainment industry, whether it is gospel driven or not, still lends itself to the challenge of competition. So it will always be a balancing act to manage the motive of profit, the instrumentality of the art form to meet customer's tastes, the aesthetic values, and the missional quality, but this does not at all mean these forms should be given up. All forms of art can nurture raw talent. They give youth something constructive to do and they bring new forms of community together.

With the Groove Awards, Kuria says they have learned to anticipate the potentially dark side of the industry. They therefore have put mechanisms in place to minimize the possibility of fallout. First, the quality of the gospel and content production is vetted on several levels. All submissions are invited from the musicians themselves, and the rules are that they must be high-quality gospel songs. Musicians have to be recognized for their Christian walk—and this is where a conservative Christian environment helps, because Kenyans will not vote for a compromising Christian. If content is submitted by a musician who has been involved in moral scandal, their music is not nominated. The Groove committee has also appointed industry gatekeepers, successful older musicians from the previous era, to walk with young musicians. They coach the annual winners so that they remain true to gospel values in the midst of their newfound fame. The committee also challenges the popular young winners to extend their influence beyond music by engaging in social activism and mentoring fresh talent in their base communities. This is not a foolproof plan, but it was a much-needed shift in the Kenyan music scene. Mulei has gone on to expand his reach through a creative production and management company with state-of-the-art equipment, professional personnel, and unique and experiential marketing concepts. His company has run some of the largest events in Kenya, including the celebration of fifty years of independence.

IMAGINING STRUCTURAL TRANSFORMATION:
FRONTLINE INITIATIVES

The change of status from ordinary people to fearless influencers and the movement's engagement in activism eventually leads to transformational work in social justice and the improvement of life conditions for those on the margins. Earlier I talked about how some churches were focused on providing services to society, while others were focused only on personal evangelism. Each of these was a noble activity; the problem was in the separation of the social and spiritual spheres, as though the two were opposed to each other. A related and more serious problem was that much of this activity, whether social action or evangelism, was rooted in attitudes and structures borrowed from the outside, not in conscious ownership and agency by the local people, which is why the younger generation did not identify with what was happening on either side.

The real impact of an evangelically revitalized society comes when the transformed people "own" the problems of their world. They see all their life, all that they do, and all their resources as essential to solving those problems. This is what Muriithi aims for at the "compelled" stage of the journey. It means the church can get directly involved transforming significant sectors, because every member is compelled to see their life as an extension of Christ's love for the world. People become invested in neighborhood and government decisions and policies that affect the less fortunate. They start volunteer societies, schools, and clinics. The fullest expression of an evangelical revitalization movement is systemic transformation of society by ongoing application of gospel values and practices in that wider society. This takes time and undoubtedly Mavuno has a ways to go before this is achieved. Yet this is the goal that Mavuno aims for, and as seen in the entertainment industry, the ship is already turning. There are other initiatives started by members of the Mavuno community that are slowly making an impact. I will discuss two of these here, Transform Kenya and Freedom Behind Bars, to elaborate more on the transformation of structural justice.

Transform Kenya: A vision to change Kenya's political culture. In chapter two, I discussed the violence that rocked Kenya in January 2008 following marred general elections. The cities and towns of Mombasa,

Nairobi, Naivasha, Nakuru, Eldoret, and Kisumu were the worst affected with deaths and displacements. While Kofi Annan resolved the stalemate politically, many churches attended to the welfare of the affected. From March 7 to 17, Mavuno pastors led two hundred pastors of the evangelical middle-class churches of Nairobi in a welfare, prayer, and reconciliation caravan called Msafara Wheels of Hope. Thousands of Christians in the region would join in prayer marches at hot spots of violence, then distribute food and hygiene packs to victims.

Amid other overarching political priorities, Msafara did not receive widespread media publicity, if any. However, that nationwide caravan was a moment of awakening for the churches in the city, especially Muriithi and the other Mavuno pastors. They recognized that regardless of ethnic differences, distance, and denominational or charismatic emphasis, churches—found in every town and city—held a special role in the reconstruction, cohesion, and inspiration of young people toward a positive future. It was from the crucible of near war that Mavuno's vision for the millennial generation across the nation and throughout Africa became crystal clear. Soon after they returned to Nairobi, Muriithi led the church in South C to relocate to spacious grounds to increase Mavuno's capacity to reach out to the city and build a culture-defining church.

One of the later outcomes was a dream to transform political culture in the long term in the form of a frontline initiative known as Transform Kenya. Along with Muriithi, the other key leader of Msafara was Simon Mbevi, who was at the time a care pastor at Mavuno. Just a little younger than Muriithi, and trained as a lawyer, Mbevi was nationally connected to clergy around the country through the Prayer Trust Network he had founded years earlier. He mobilized all the clergy he knew to meet the caravan of hope at each town. Afterward he felt compelled to resign from formal pastoral ministry and engage the national crisis of leadership that had led the country to the verge of political violence. Mbevi also had political experience. In 2002 he ran for member of Parliament for the Makueni constituency, where he was loved by the local people, but he was cheated out of the position through underhanded deals. That attempt taught him valuable lessons about how politics worked. He would later surmise that the entrenched political culture, habits, and gatekeepers are impossible to change overnight. So he founded Transform Kenya to prepare for long-term transformation.

From his experience, Mbevi says that the media and arts sectors of society are at the front door of culture, where they readily influence popular opinion. Yet media and arts also quickly shift allegiances with the winds of change. They are both easy to change and easy to manipulate. As seen in the stories of Mbugua, A-Star, and Mulei above, Mavuno has had significant influence in these sectors of society. On the other hand, political and government processes are much harder to influence because they are at the back end of culture, entrenched in bureaucracies of state and backed by powerfully resourced gatekeepers who then control media to sway public opinion. The few well-meaning Christians that make it to political office seem to be co-opted by the mess because it takes far more than good intentions to reform a negatively entrenched political culture. It would take a transformation of the entire value system, which starts with the preparation of leaders long before they vie for political office. Even then, to change bad laws, corruption, impunity, and stifling bureaucracies takes much work and strategy behind the scenes for a long time. It may take more than a generation.

This, then, is the greater logic of Mavuno's efforts to transform all the other sectors of society, which are sandwiched between the front end of media and cultural industries and the entrenched political culture on the back end. Health, education, economics, environment, and even the church are sometimes used and manipulated, sometimes strengthened, by what happens between the juggernauts of politics and media.

This also is the logic of Mbevi's Transform Kenya. His goal is to use the platform of successful churches—such as Mavuno, but also the Anglican Church, Catholic Church, and many of the Pentecostal churches that are now awakened to the challenge of dysfunctional politics and the social sphere—to inspire the emergence of responsible leaders for the next generation. He starts by challenging men to rise up to leadership at home, in the marketplace, and eventually in the political arena. To this end Transform Kenya runs several programs. "Man Enough" addresses the lack of awareness among men about their leadership duties, starting with the home. This is evidenced in what Mbevi and Muriithi refer to as the crisis of fatherlessness.

In one outreach to prisons, Mbevi and his team carried out research which showed that 80 percent of men in the prison had troubled relationships with their fathers, what he calls "father wounds." These were absentee, abusive, or uninvolved fathers. The men in turn end up in jail or pass on these problems to their families and workplaces. This lack of leadership awareness is also evidenced in lifestyles that sabotage the welfare of men's spheres of influence, such as excessive consumption of alcohol and keeping several women while neglecting family duties.

Transform Kenya runs curriculum-based programs for men and boys. Man Enough is unapologetically a vision for mentoring men. The contemporary focus on equality has tended to presume that empowering one group or the other, men or women, necessarily means the negligence of the other group. According to Mbevi, the overemphasis on the empowerment of girls in the 1990s was part of the sweeping global influence on local African cultures. It is true that girls had been neglected, but those who championed them ended up alienating the boys. So while girl-empowerment programs rightfully succeeded in raising a generation of successful women, the boys did not have role models or aspirations. Many girls went to school and were inspired to be all that they could be, but because the boys were left behind, the empowered women found there were no responsible husbands for them. Many of the empowered women are struggling to raise families alone after their husbands abdicate responsibility. Mbevi's vision in the present moment is to reach the Kenyan millennial man and reeducate him to rise up to responsibility. The Man Enough program originally started at Mavuno but has grown to recruit men from diverse churches and train them through a curriculum, coaching them in personal, family, and community responsibility and legacy building. "Lead to Serve" is another tailored coaching initiative for men in specific leadership roles, and "Boys to Men" reaches teenage boys in select high schools to bridge the fatherhood gap, helping them to transition to responsible young adulthood.

In focusing on men, Mbevi says he has no utopian expectation that this will change the country in the short term, but he looked at the ineffectiveness of the short-term "fix-it" initiatives that tend to come from the West—such as hit-and-run conferences built around a successful business or church persona—and knew he would have to invest in generational transformation. In particular, he and Muriithi are skeptical of "spiritual" programs that assume that a single conference or the occasional camp or giving away free books will help. Even when they are well intentioned, many of these attempts fail to connect with the cultural nuances of the identity and needs of men in Kenya, and they fail to engage churches at the vital grassroots level. Mbevi is working to build a grassroots transformational movement, inspiring homegrown mentorship of men, so that in another generation, these men and their children will emerge as a cohort of good leaders in all sectors of society. Short-term transformation is already evident among the men who have participated in Man Enough and Lead to Serve, but the real impact is expected to be felt in the long run. Mbevi believes that the work of Transform Kenya will succeed through the involvement of churches, so he spends significant time speaking to men in churches and securing the support of church leaders to mobilize their men. Like other frontline initiatives, Transform Kenya has a base of core supporters at Mavuno Church. Mbevi has also been warmly embraced by several older, middle-class churches—All Saints Cathedral (Anglican Church), Don Bosco Catholic Church (Nairobi Diocese), Deliverance Church Umoja (neo-Pentecostal), Life Spring and Karura communities, Nairobi Baptist, and CITAM churches. Interestingly, he downplays the historical denominational differences among these churches, asserting that Western conflicts of earlier generations should not be perpetuated in Africa. Mbevi also has a growing international profile as a trainer on issues about men.

Freedom Behind Bars: Rehabilitating prisoners. While Mbevi is building long-term grassroots transformation among boys and men, Frank Mutua is running an initiative geared toward short- and medium-term intervention in the societal problem of Kenyan prisons. Mutua started Freedom Behind Bars after his brother was arrested and jailed for a petty offence. Until then, Mutua, like most Kenyans, was indifferent to the plight of prisoners. When he visited his brother, he was moved by the sorry conditions of jail. He knew that despite the misdemeanor, his brother was a good family man with a wife and two children. Through his brother's experience he began to see the humanity of prisoners, and he investigated further into the conditions of Kenya's prisons. Following this incident, some prison wardens learned that Mutua was from Mavuno Church, which was already well known in prison circles. Mavuno had previously visited several prisons around Nairobi, donating essentials such as beds, mattresses, and toiletries to prison inmates. Mavuno also used to run an annual outreach event in prisons called "Spread the Love," which involved rehabilitating the prison facilities and donating supplies for wardens.

After the incident with his brother, the chief warden of the Kiambu Prison on the outskirts of Nairobi called Mutua into her office and asked if he would bring Mavuno Church to visit her prisoners. Mutua, who was then volunteering with Mavuno's life-group department, mobilized several life groups to collect supplies for Kiambu Prison. They made a series of visits, each time donating much-needed hygiene supplies and counseling prisoners. Then they realized the real need was to help the prisoners rebuild their self-worth and prepare to rejoin society, so they began discussions with the Mavuno pastors about the best way to do that. The pastors recommended Mizizi, which would lead prisoners to connect with Christ, connect with a sense of purpose, and build community even behind bars. It was daring, but they decided to try it. In early 2011 they secured permission to start a Mizizi class to rehabilitate willing prisoners. Ninety prisoners signed up for two initial classes. The life-groups department at Mavuno mobilized a large cohort of Mizizi volunteers to facilitate these classes and embarked on a journey to help prison wardens reform both petty and hardened criminals. In stories that read like that of the biblical Joseph, dozens of inmates were transformed and made into prison prefects over their fellow inmates. Some had their sentences commuted, others are preaching to fellow prisoners behind bars. For most that have taken the Mizizi classes, the hopelessness that goes with incarceration is gone. Prison wardens from other prisons, surprised to hear about the transformation of inmates, began requesting not just Mavuno visits with support supplies, but also Mizizi classes for their prisoners and for the wardens themselves. According to Mutua, prison officials have now opened the doors wide for Mavuno as Mizizi rehabilitates regular and hardened criminals and as Mavuno life groups continue to visit the prisoners regularly—thus the name, Freedom Behind Bars. As of the end of 2014, Mizizi classes were running in five of the nine prisons in the country, including Shimo la

Tewa at the coast, nearly five hundred kilometers (310 miles) away. Not to mention that Mutua also runs a business to earn a living; he does Freedom Behind Bars in his downtime with the help of a large team of Mavuno volunteers. The funds for this initiative come from the volunteers and their networks. Some volunteers have taken on added responsibility to help ex-prisoners reenter society, connecting them to halfway houses and helping them find jobs.

GOING GLOBAL: TO WIN A CITY . . . AND CHANGE THE WORLD

Mavuno Church is pursuing a local, regional, and global vision, to "win the city, take the continent, and change the world." *Glocalization* is a word that describes a localized vision going global. After local people have recovered from the shock of global forces, created their own vision, and succeeded in transforming parts of their world, they join the global highway to spread their influence abroad. The vision to plant churches is rooted in Muriithi's passion to reach the millennials and the fragile middle class emerging across Africa. Muriithi says that, given the egotistic nature of the middle-class lifestyle itself, other groups seeking a mindshare of this class, and the entrenched problems of the continent, it will take a lot more than government reform and capitalist-driven economic growth to secure Africa on positive footing. It will require the intervention of a people who are deeply interested in the welfare of the continent and whose motive is other than political and economic self-interest. It will take communities that are transformed by God's Word, who have a vision for their continent.

Muriithi believes that only the church can truly change Africa for the better. He affirms that, for all its inconsistencies, the church has been deeply involved in the formation of twentieth-century Africa, and there is more work for it in the twenty-first century. But for this to happen, the twentieth-century church has to update its vision to reach the millennial generation. This passion drives Mavuno's vision to "plant a culture-defining church in every capital city of Africa by the year 2035." This passionate concern is expressed in a signature song written by worship director Kanji Mbugua, "Africa, rise up stand up, this is your moment, this is your time!"

The sun is shining in this land
It reaches out across the land,
The shadows lapse, now it's bright
And the clouds of night have passed
Across the nations people rise and
Put aside their prejudice
Guns are silent no more wars and the land has been restored . . .
Africa rise up, stand up this is your moment, this is your time.

Mavuno Church has modeled how to reach millennials in Nairobi. Yet the goal is not to replicate the Mavuno Marathon model in the same way around Africa. The Marathon as configured at the original Mavuno may serve as a tool to get started, but with time local congregations, under the direction of leaders who are problem solving, generating contextual ideas, and raising young new leaders, will take the shape of their own context. For instance, in Nairobi Mavuno has planted six satellite churches in addition to the central campus. Each of these, while following the model of the Marathon in organizational structure, has found a different niche and methods to reach slightly different demographics in their location. Mavuno Downtown, planted by Kyama Mugambi in 2006, meets close to the University of Nairobi and reaches intellectually astute university students. One of their touchstone programs is called Campus Trend, which helps students build integrity while still in university so that their fearless influence begins early. Mavuno Mashariki was initially planted by Nairobi Chapel to reach the area known as Eastlands. Its unique niche is to address the rampant alcohol- and drug-addiction problem among youth in eastern Nairobi. Mavuno Kampala, started in 2012 as the first international church plant of Mavuno, is the first young-adult congregation in Kampala. It grew quickly, so that by 2015 it had about five hundred members and was planting two other churches. Other budding congregations in African cities include Blantyre, Lusaka, and Kigali. These are led by young couples who have trained through Mavuno's leadership pipeline and were then commissioned to plant while in turn raising leaders in these new cities. Mavuno Berlin (Germany) existed as an Evangelical Lutheran congregation, but its numbers had declined to the point of closing, like Nairobi Chapel in the 1980s. Following a series of relational contacts, the elders ceded the church to Mavuno's leadership. A young German couple, Nancy and Daniel Fleschig, spent three years at Mavuno in Nairobi as pastoral leadership trainees. In 2012 they were commissioned to lead Mavuno Berlin, which is now on a positive growth curve. The Mavuno Berlin model of revitalizing older congregations may be the method that Mavuno will use to plant more churches in Europe with the vision of reaching the millennial demographic there.

Church planters start out at the internship level. A rigorous selection process for interns is designed to ensure they have a vibrant relationship with God, a clear sense of call into ministry, leadership potential, and willingness to learn. The process of planting a new international church takes more than a year before a congregation starts. Every year a team of interns goes on a short-term mission trip to a designated country to scout out possibilities of a church among millennials. Then a team from the church-planting department (including life groups) that "adopted" the country follows. They build relationships with young adults in the business community, university, media and entertainment industries, and often with leaders of existing churches in the area. Among these new contacts a core group is taught the Mavuno Church vision and begins a Mizizi class. That first graduating class becomes the catalyst for a second and third classes, usually from their networks of friends and families. This core grows into a critical mass to start a church plant—anywhere between thirty and a hundred people. This is how Mavuno planted churches in Kampala, Uganda, Kigali, Rwanda, Blantyre, Malawi and Lusaka, Zambia, and Addis Ababa, with similar plans to start churches in other African capital cities.

As the buzz continues to spread about Mavuno's unique model, the influence extends beyond church planting. When he started out at South C, Muriithi was little known and disparaged as a youth pastor. Now he is frequently sought out to help churches understand young adults, and he serves informally as a mentor and formally as a leadership coach on these matters. He has informal partnerships with many churches in Nairobi, such as the International Christian Center, led by Philip Kitoto and Edward Munene; the Purpose Center, led by Julian Kyula; and even older Pentecostal churches, such as Deliverance Church in Umoja, led by Bishop J. B. Masinde; and House of Grace, led by David Muriithi. Muriithi welcomes these opportunities, insisting that we must rally as many people as possible to reach the growing youth bulge. Africa's transformation will take every church that can be mobilized, including the older churches that are willing to learn to engage millennials. The "Fearless Network" is Mavuno's open source for sharing the strategies that Mavuno has learned the hard way so that other churches can understand the urgency and get on board.

Mavuno Church has received international attention as well. One thriving international partnership is with a church in Orange County, California. In 2009 Mavuno's worship band played at Mariners Church in Irvine during their tour of the United States. Following the tour, a relationship began through which Mariners's senior leaders, including their pastors, visited Nairobi on several occasions to learn how Mavuno was reaching a younger generation. Mariners hired an African pastor, Christian Mungai, with the blessing of Mavuno Church, to lead their global initiatives. Mungai has transformed the way Mariners does international outreach, moving away from the old model of sending finances and short-term teams abroad, to an actual partnership where short-term teams, money, projects, and other mission activities are subservient to a cultivated relationship.

As part of its commitment to learn from an African church, Mariners Church adopted the Mavuno Marathon for its own congregation, including their own adapted version of the Mavuno mission statement: "Transforming ordinary people into passionate followers of Jesus Christ, courageously shaping culture" (as seen in figure 5.1). Mariners has also adopted Mizizi, which they call "Rooted," and adapted it for an American context. They have taken their entire congregation of twelve thousand members through it. Each year Mavuno sends several staff members to Mariners to facilitate some of these Mizizi classes. Like at Mavuno, running Mizizi requires a large number of volunteers, which means a much larger percentage of their congregation is now engaging their spiritual gifts. Together Mavuno and Mariners have built a network of at least two hundred churches in the United States and beyond—in China, Egypt, Haiti, Mexico, and Sri Lanka—all of which are variously sharing Mavuno's resources to reach and disciple younger generations everywhere. Mizizi has also been translated into French, Chinese, and Spanish.

Figure 5.1. Mariners Church Transformational Loop

IT'S A WRAP: MEET THE AFROPOLITANS

Do you remember Yonatan, my researcher friend who came to visit Mavuno Church with me in 2012 (see this book's introduction)? After we had just attended a main service in the tent, he asked if I could take him to the adult church. That is because the crowd he saw that day not only looked young in age, but the spruce, polish, and flush wasn't what he expected of an African congregation.

Meet the new Afropolitans.[8]

---

[8]This term *Afropolitans* was popularized by Taiye Selasi in a 2005 magazine article describing young diaspora Africans who, as children of immigrant or international working parents, had grown up in global metropolitan cities. The Afropolitans of Selasi's reckoning were presented

You would not take them seriously as a church if you were looking for women dressed to the nines in African fabric or were expecting disheveled down-and-outs in search of comfort from a pastor. You are in the wrong church if you expect the preacher to yell her voice hoarse, or if you expect the annual meeting to drag along through three hours of building committee minutes. As a matter of fact, the annual general meeting at Mavuno is quite the opposite: it's called Leader's Day and it draws in every person that lends their skills, gifts, and passion to the ministries of the church, which is just about everybody who has taken a Mizizi class and stayed in a life group.

If you are looking for a church where weekly routine and self-identity blends with Sunday camaraderie, you have found your club. Spiritually, the measured passion of the twenty-five to thirty minutes of singing and prayer might betray the fact that many who come to Mavuno Church for the two-hour-service are still trying to figure it out. The Friday night prayer and healing will reveal personal lifestyle battles still being laid at the foot of the cross, but these are no longer debilitating sources of anguish drowned out in drunken stupors at neighborhood bars. The annual preaching calendar is organized into seasons of reeducational discipleship, covering a wide range of issues relating to career, personal goals, church community, praying for the nation, evangelism, managing finances, celebrating life—all of which, seen collectively, are shaping a movement, whose synergy is expected to transcend individual accomplishments.

Financially, most of Mavuno's Afropolitans do not have permanent jobs, but they have plenty of creative hustles, smalltime contracts in service industries, gigs in information technology, mass and social media, business coaching, culinary arts, and photography. To see how they are professionally engaged and connected, one only has to follow their LinkedIn networks. They connect, support one another, and draw in others, so that church is as much a networking as a discipleship community, a new family, and they

---

as trying to come to terms with the multiple identities of their global legacies, as well as the contradictions in their mother continent. I use this word to describe the similar, freshly self-conscious young adult who is networked in places like Mavuno but is also found in other elective-affinity cultural sites around the city. This young adult is also regionally and globally connected through technology and travel. See Taiye Selasi, "Bye-Bye Babar," *The LIP Magazine*, March 3, 2005, http://thelip.robertsharp.co.uk/?p=76.

extend the same energies to their chosen volunteer responsibilities in church. Whatever they earn, the annual finance sermon series at Mavuno has taught them to live within their means: to budget, save, and invest in more creative hustles. Significantly for Mavuno, they faithfully give a monthly tithe, enough to ensure that Mavuno runs on a budget of several million shillings (roughly US$30,000) a month, can afford to purchase permanent property after a relatively short but intense capital campaign, and will continue to plant new churches in the region.

Socially, Mavuno Afropolitans no longer represent the sharp tribal divides of their parents' generation. They intermarry across ethnic communities and use blended African names for their children. English remains their language of business, but they do very well in Sheng, that practical urban mélange of Swahili, English, and local dialects. If you go to one of their weekly life groups, not only will you sing global contemporary Christian music alongside homegrown genres, you'll also find business literature and lifestyle hacks being discussed alongside Mavuno curriculums. There is even the odd book club. Yet these are no longer disparate attempts at self-help—they are bound together by a reason. There are still stories of family or work dramas, and there are dropouts. Nevertheless they keep these in perspective of the graver problems in the world.

Their social-media posts suggest that life is not altogether rosy in personal, city, and country affairs. Personal achievement is tempered by the contradictions of the bustling city. Intense hopes are embodied in gleaming asphalt highways constructed by Chinese contractors, paid by Western loans, and clogged with remodeled Japanese cars during rush hour. The glistening shopping malls in lush suburbs are selling merchandise imported from Dubai because the country's industrial area merely repackages cheap ware sourced from China and hawked by jobless graduates on the streets of low-income settlements. The NGO-esque and tourism service industries that flush the country with liquid cash are ready to evaporate like mist at the slightest stroke of misfortune. And the poorly serviced low-income settlements continue to swell with rising birthrates and migrants from rural communities.

All of this is to say that the Afropolitan class, although freshly self-conscious and empowered at places like Mavuno Church, is ambitious and optimistic in the world, but as they move into middle adulthood, they know there is more work cut out for them. Thus for Mavuno's leadership and for those of us reflecting on Mavuno's journey, the story cannot end just yet. In the next chapter, we will think through these issues theologically.

6

First-World Problems Worth Solving

Christianity's Ambiguity with Modernity

FIRST-WORLD SUCCESS, THIRD-WORLD PROBLEMS

The modern era of economic growth, spanning from the industrial revolution through the twentieth century, has brought high standards of living to Western societies. The majority of adults in the United States, Canada, Western Europe, Japan, Australia, and New Zealand have a per capita income in excess of US$55,000 per year, while the comparative income of those in the poorest nations, such as Niger, is $935.[1] In light of this privileged status, Western street idiom is accustomed to dismissing trivial issues with the phrase "first-world problems." The dismissal suggests that in view of the poorest countries where people are dying of hunger, disease, and conflict, those in developed nations should not whine over petty problems. When the privileged think they are suffering, they should imagine, for instance, a Ugandan boy turned into a child soldier by the evil warlord Joseph Kony and instead count their blessings. Or so the logic goes.

The sentimentality of the phrase "first-world problems" is charming in its attempt to restrain sob stories in a world where structures of law and order work, where necessities of life and medical care are within reach, and where grocery stores are extravagantly stocked. Yet these characteristics that make the first world "first" have implications worth thinking about, not least for Christians.

---

[1]World Bank, "GDP per Capita, PPP (Current International $)," http://data.worldbank.org /indicator/NY.GDP.PCAP.PP.CD (accessed March 12, 2018).

The labels *first, second,* and *third world* come from the era after the world wars, between 1947 and 1991. The first world comprised those countries whose economies were already ahead of others through a capitalist mode of production. The second world, known for its socialism, represented those countries marked by state ownership of all means of economic production. The third world included countries that opted for a "third way," different from capitalist and socialist states.[2] These "third way" countries were also emerging from colonial domination. They chose not to be allied with either of the other two, as they were fixed on self-determination. To fast-track their infrastructural development, however, these nations were granted large amounts of foreign aid through Western agencies such as the IMF and the World Bank or were controlled through the Cold War. Unfortunately, foreign aid eventually became a ball and chain, as intended autonomy morphed into a sinister dependency.[3] A combination of factors, including the infamous economic fallouts beginning in the 1970s, Cold War–related civil conflicts, and debilitating diseases such as HIV/AIDS, malaria, and tuberculosis, curtailed development agendas. The ill-advised structural adjustment programs and heavy debt obligations to successive generations made matters worse. The label "third world" became synonymous with poverty and suffering, and the conscience-stricken Western world evolved into not only an aid donor but also a humanitarian benefactor of the deprived third world.

The third world, especially Africa, is scarcely able to live down this antipathetic label. Yet as we have seen, a new narrative is overriding the pessimism. Although development agendas were not wildly successful, the cumulative and collective impact of decades of aid and development investment—plus the sheer sweat of ordinary Africans—has produced a measure of forward movement, including expansion in education, stabilizing of democracies and economies, increase in modern infrastructure, and budding technological innovations. The millennium development goals (MDGs), one of the measures used to mark visible reduction in poverty

---

[2]Jeffrey Sachs, *The End of Poverty: Economic Possibilities for Our Time* (New York: Penguin, 2005), 48.
[3]Dambisa Moyo, *Dead Aid: Why Aid Is Not Working and How There Is a Better Way for Africa* (New York: Farrar, Straus and Giroux, 2010).

between 1990 and 2015, make a good case for the point at hand.[4] Although
they engendered cynicism and, in some cases, remained a mirage, the
MDGs' global mobilization was successful in showing that more than a
billion people have moved out of extreme poverty in the twenty-five-year
period. The youth bulge in Africa, as well as the corresponding young-adult
bulge in Asian and Latin American countries, is a key indicator. Everywhere
child mortality rates have dropped drastically; literacy rates are now at an
all-time high of over 80 percent. Across Africa and globally at least five
billion people have reached the first rung of economic development, one
step above extreme poverty. According to economists, at least 5.7 of the
world's 7.2 billion people now live in countries where life expectancy is on
the rise. The incidence of extreme poverty is shrinking, both in absolute
numbers and as a proportion of the world's population. Economist Jeffrey
Sachs maintains that economic development is real and widespread.[5]

I cite the global developments here to make a point. Whatever theories
we would apply concerning modernization in Africa and the rest of the
Global South—and there are quite a few books on that—even the most
skeptical should be able to see that transition is taking place from impov-
erished, primordial worlds into those which will increasingly resemble the
Western world. It is not a fait accompli, but it's heading there.

Of all people, Western Christians should have seen this transition out
of poverty coming. They were in the business of transforming African,
Asian, and Latin American life long before the interventions of guilt-driven
and self-interested Western governments. Right from the start, missionaries
discovered that they could not preach the gospel without attending to
material needs. Scholars of world Christianity such as Lamin Sanneh observe this fact well.[6] By the time missionaries came to the Global South,

---

[4]In 2000 world leaders committed to "spare no effort to free fellow humanity from the abject
and dehumanizing conditions of extreme poverty." This was translated into a framework of eight
goals with wide-ranging practical steps and innovative partnerships. The targets included erad-
icating extreme poverty and hunger, achieving universal primary education, promoting gender
equality, empowering women, improving maternal health and reducing child mortality, combating
HIV/AIDS, ensuring environmental sustainability. Accordingly the MDGs helped to lift more
than one billion people out of extreme poverty. United Nations, "United Nations Millennium
Development Goals," www.un.org/millenniumgoals (accessed May 24, 2016).
[5]Sachs, The End of Poverty, 51.
[6]Lamin O. Sanneh, Disciples of All Nations: Pillars of World Christianity, Oxford Studies in World
Christianity (New York: Oxford University Press, 2008), 224-25.

it was assumed that the gospel that had made Western nations prosperous could do the same for other nations. Missionaries therefore devoted themselves to providing medicine and education as accompaniments to preaching. Granted, their rationale was to lift people out of "backwardness" and lead them to recognize that the source of these blessings was God, so they would worship him. Still, it is to the credit of missionaries, at least in Africa, that by the time most colonized nations achieved independence, there was an educated cohort to take over from colonial settlers.[7] In postcolonial Africa, Christianity has always had a special relevance in bettering the social conditions of local communities. Christianity has taken the lead particularly in getting people out of shadows of isolation and into the orbit of universal progress. It has taken time, but to a degree, this has worked. A good example of the outcome of long-range investment in education and social concern is the rise of a higher middle-class demographic in Anglophone Africa, in contrast to former French and Portuguese regions, which are yet to build a notable middle class.[8] A visible result of the cumulative investment in child-educational sponsorship, humanitarian aid, and development aid is the stabilizing of populations now turning into the current youth bulge.[9]

---

[7]For a balanced view on the relationship between missionaries and colonial governments and settlers, see Brian Stanley, *The Bible and the Flag: Protestant Missions and British Imperialism in the Nineteenth and Twentieth Centuries* (Leicester, England: Apollos, 1990).

[8]Woodberry's research in Anglophone countries in Africa demonstrated that historically and statistically, missionaries that put a lot of effort into promoting mass education, printing, newspapers, voluntary organizations, and reforms hugely influenced the rise and spread of stable democracies. This explains the variation in democratic stability of sub-Saharan African countries. Countries that had more Protestant missions have on the whole had a more positive experience with democracy and capitalist economies than those outside of that orbit. See Robert D. Woodberry, "The Missionary Roots of Liberal Democracy," *American Political Science Review* 106, no. 2 (May 2012): 244-74.

[9]Even beyond mission work, the Western church has contributed resources to the development agenda. Despite the reticence of evangelical Christianity to engage socially for a significant part of the twentieth century, parachurch organizations such as World Vision, World Relief, Care, Oxfam, Compassion International, TearFund, Micah Challenge, Catholic Relief Services, International Justice Mission, as well as individual benevolence through short-term mission groups, have engaged in humanitarian and developmental work for several decades. Child educational sponsorship, for instance, has been a leading form of direct aid from wealthy country households to children in developing countries. A detailed study of twelve years of child sponsorship programs in six countries showed a positive impact on the educational, employment, and leadership outcomes of child sponsorship. See Bruce Wydick, Paul Glewwe, and Laine Rutledge, "Does International Child Sponsorship Work? A Six-Country Study of

148   MEGACHURCH CHRISTIANITY RECONSIDERED

There is a baby here that is not to be thrown out with the bath water. Yes, it is true that the kind of capitalism-driven economic development in today's world engenders its own pathologies, as pointed out in chapter two. While the capitalist market itself is inevitable as a preexisting social dynamic of modern life, the kind of entrepreneurial capitalism celebrated in Max Weber's Protestant work ethic—with its core values of hard work, asceticism, deferred gratification, savings, and philanthropic altruism—has been replaced by hyperconsumption egged on by marketing hype. It is also true that there are still a billion people living in absolute poverty around the world and that there are still significant levels of instability in parts of the world and high levels of inequality between the rich and the poor. Yet this does not preclude the measure of visible economic success pulling sections of the non-Western world into the range of middle-class incomes similar to those of the first world. As we have seen, more of the world has a higher life expectancy, falling infant-mortality rates, greater educational attainment, increasing access to water and sanitation, better incomes, and higher capacity to acquire consumer goods. First-world problems will not just be first-world problems for long; they are becoming global realities. In Africa, even if all we have is a youth bulge, it takes no stretch of the imagination to see that this demographic may well become a middle class, because the world has come knocking afresh in pursuit of economic opportunities, and Africans are no longer passive in this global game. The human capital required to turn the renewed global interest into a world that looks more like the first world, where people have access to food, health, and a wide variety of consumer goods, lies within reach of a generation.

WESTERN CHRISTIANITY'S ANTITHESIS
TO MATERIALITY

Herein lies the rub with first-world problems worth solving. Although they helped lift society up, Christian missionaries and the churches that grew up after their era had one primary goal: to get people to heaven. They did not reflect on the logic of where else their message led. They did not

Impacts on Adult Life Outcomes," *Journal of Political Economy* 121, no. 2 (April 1, 2013): 393-436.

consider the relationship between the Christian message and the intermediate destination to which it leads, that is, the success that comes with the
stability of a Christian life, which then has a ripple effect on family,
community, work disciplines, and the discovery of new priorities that
improve the life of the individual and their social worlds. In other words,
if the conditions are right, becoming a Christian potentially set one up to
be prosperous, relative to the social context. Instead, as Maia Green reports
in her research on historic mission denominations in Tanzania, "Whichever
mission and irrespective of the kinds of technological innovations that
missionaries introduced, the certainties of colonial Christianity were
arguably antithetical to western understandings of modernity as a progressive
agenda."[10] Green observes what is true of Christianity everywhere: it intended to convert people for the other world of heaven, not to turn them
into successful modern people. And so the motive has remained.

Whereas poverty, deprivation, and injustice continue to be the primary
arena of Christians' social intervention, by and large Global-South Christianity (except perhaps in Korea) has retained the Western reticence to
engage with the positive consequences of material progress, whether political,
economic, or social. For instance, it has been a painful process for much
of Christianity in Africa to step up to challenge the dysfunction of African
politics. The churches only demanded inclusive politics in the last decades
of the twentieth century, but by then most African nations had suffered
under decades of bad politics—under rulers who had been educated as
Christians in mission schools. But this hurdle has been jumped, and most
churches in Africa and Latin America, including Pentecostals, now have
some modicum of political and civic engagement.

The issue at hand in the present century is what to do with increasingly
prosperous economic circumstances and all the trappings—a first-world
problem whose theological issues are worth solving. How are Africans,
Asians, and Latin Americans joining the amorphous middle-class status
to relate their improved economic and social status to their identity as
Christians? How are they also to cope with its individual (psychological),
communal (cultural), and societal (national/global) tensions? As much as

---

[10]Maia Green, *Priests, Witches, and Power: Popular Christianity After Mission in Southern Tanzania*
(New York: Cambridge University Press, 2003), 3.

it has grown into and lived in the middle of affluence, the Western church has never really resolved this question for itself. Western Christianity, like its missionaries, has preached either to get people into heaven or to build a more progressive society; one path is an all-out disavowal of modernity and the other is an all-out embrace of modernity. Both create a niche in the modernization process, but neither offers a rational critique of it.

In the second half of the twentieth century, two theological issues added to the hesitation to think about the relationship between the success of Western Christians in middle-income brackets, their lifestyle culture, and the Christian faith. One was a legitimate concern for the poor and the voiceless. This concern was shaped by liberation theologies from the Global South, which heightened awareness of structural evil of certain socio-political and economic arrangements originating from the outside. Varieties of Western Christians were also haunted by the conditions of social inequality, marginalization, and discrimination in their own worlds. So they did not accept in toto that they were a prosperous society. Of course, they knew they were prosperous, but the best way to assuage a restless conscience is to give toward the improvement of conditions of the world's suffering masses—though they usually did so at arm's length while fleeing from the troubled core of their own cities. The century-long gulf between liberal and conservative Christians, one group emphasizing the progressive social gospel and the other evangelistic proclamation, exacerbated this dis-ease. To their credit, beyond their own borders their concern for the voiceless was expressed in a variety of humanitarian efforts for people suffering across the Global South, whether in Latin America's revolutionary politics, Africa's diseases, or Asia's drug and human-trafficking problem. A myriad of Western-funded NGOs, trusts, and parachurch works appeared all over the Global South. Western Christians have tended to give liberally to help the rest of the world. An outpouring of humanitarian and development-oriented literature rightly accompanies Western generosity. Yet if these writers raise issues that are pertinent, the conversations are not entirely connected with the key question for Western Christians—how to be Christianly modern.

There is no dispute about one critically essential aspect of the gospel. A theology of helping the poor has been necessary wherever people are suffering marginalization, poverty, and their consequences. However, the application of its logic across the world and in subsequent decades has resulted in nervous nail biting among Christians wherever socioeconomic success has emerged as shared societal reality. Christians are edgy both about the need to help the poor and about the focus on creating and living with wealth. They don't know what to do either with success or the absence of it. Damned if you do; damned if you don't. Christian literature on wealth creation, missions and money, and generosity doesn't usually help new Christian communities understand that the way forward is neither the ascetic denunciation of success nor an uncritical embrace of all the wealth and success one can get—though these two attitudes seem to be the default for many Christians. What is needed is an ethical vision of success generated through all the products (the city, technology) and processes (capitalist market, modern politics) of modernization in all their constructive (human progress, prosperity) and shadow (alienation, meaninglessness, marginalization of the most vulnerable) sides. It is also necessary to generate an ethical vision of the places where this success is most obvious, the metropolitan city in both its ideological and spatial configurations. This is what is missing as part of a consistent vision for living in the contemporary, modernized world.

The other problem is the absence of a consistent articulation of the relationship between mainstream theology and prosperity theology, its uncharacteristic offspring, which has taken root in recent decades. I call it uncharacteristic because the fault lines between the legitimate claims of prosperity theology—material wealth and physical well-being as outcomes of a diligent Christian life—and its problems with power, greed, and abuse of spiritual authority are tensions that we find among God's people throughout the Scriptures and Christian history. Western Christian theologians have discussed this in part, but the church lacks a consistently developed theology of how to be Christianly prosperous—how to live as a Christian in a world of access to technology, style consciousness, comfort, entertainment, transient and fleeting means of communication, and so on. Successful Christians tend to idealize and idolize the few remarkable "saints" that step out of the mainstream to take up a path of downward mobility among poor communities that have no choice about their poverty. Christians have remained largely uneasy about facing up to these dynamics, especially granted the larger masses of people living without bare necessities. Yet like modernization, these are social dynamics that cannot be wished out of the world we live in. The same goes for the processes and arrangements of globalization originating from the West and sweeping into the Global South: economic, political, and cultural exchange. Much of the ink spilled about Christianity and globalization has been marked by handwringing instead of an attempt to shape the conversation in ways that equip new Christian communities to respond to and live with these inevitable crosscurrents.

Wealth, success, and prosperity as defined in first-world terms—access to food, health care, education, security, and all the freedom of choice available with these items—and now exported all over the world under the rubric of modernization is a global, twenty-first-century, Christian problem worth solving. Even the postmodern critique of modernity (that is, disillusionment with progress occasioned by modernizing processes) does not preclude a coherent theological engagement with those structures of social life introduced by modernity—the city, the market, the school, the bureaucratic state. However convoluted the ascendancy of these modernizing processes, this is now the world in which new Christian communities across the Global South are being formed. Some individuals may opt for the downwardly mobile life, and some small Christian communities may opt for monastic living, but most people want to know how to make it in a cutthroat workplace, secure a future, raise kids in the world of contemporary education structures and media, get along with strange neighbors (that is, deal with pluralism and multiculturalism), file tax returns, balance a budget, and handle whatever other mundane issues come with living, especially in the city. Christians can no longer avoid addressing materiality in the late modern world. To use millennial street-speak: "It's a thing. Deal with it."

MEGACHURCHES AND MODERNIZATION
IN THE REARVIEW MIRROR

This brings me back to megachurches. A church like Mavuno in South C found and attracted a college-educated demographic. In chapter two I painted possible scenarios for this demographic: either greater social volatility in dysfunctional nations or personal meaninglessness within a successful but socially disjointed world. Instead of joining the lament about the failure of churches, the youth's waywardness, the political malaise, or the ills of mass media, Mavuno Church fraternized with technology, business literature, developmental psychology, and the "errant" hip culture to get millennials back into wholesome community and lead them into stable lifestyles. As more people find a home within this Christianity, not just at Mavuno but in many other mega- and not-so-mega churches cropping up around the world that operate with the same logic, we begin to see that somehow the structures of modernity hold the key to engaging and re-taining those born and raised in it.

Much contemporary opinion assumes that the primary drive of mega-churches is numbers or that the way they tinker with culture is new. In fact, however, the pragmatism of a present-day megachurch like Mavuno is rooted in the form of Christianity that believes that the Great Commission carries with it an imperative to convert all people from sinners into fervent followers of Jesus. These sinners need to be reached by all means possible. This imperative and its accompanying pragmatism goes back to eighteenth-century evangelical awakenings, which were in themselves responses to profoundly disjunctive social change.[11] The preachers of the great awakenings were impelled by insight into a decaying world, a decay triggered by the incomprehensible progress of the industrial revolution, just like what we have been witnessing in Africa in the last century. When the old maps of reality had failed, young and upcoming revivalists preached a new light that unlocked immense creative energies in new generations. For instance, John Wesley, founder of Methodism, came onto the scene when English society was sick with organic disorder at the start of the industrial revolution. In the previous century, Britain had gone through repeated political and religious conflicts that had drained society. State pulpits weakly condemned the societal vices of an increasingly materi-alistic society. Wesley first challenged the poorest of the poor to discover and live up to their dignity as children of God, a message that came as a healing salve to turn a hopeless world around, and the rest is the history

---

[11]Mark A. Noll, *The Rise of Evangelicalism: The Age of Edwards, Whitefield and the Wesleys* (Downers Grove, IL: InterVarsity Press, 2010); Mark Hutchinson, *A Short History of Global Evangelicalism* (New York: Cambridge University Press, 2012).

of Methodism. In the American colonies at the time of the great revivalist Jonathan Edwards, the wheels of change were turning toward what would become the democratic American nation, but it was still a traditional world. Edwards's biographer, George Marsden, writes that New England at the time was a world of taken-for-granted hierarchical structures controlled by personal relationships and structures of patriarchy.[12] Revisionist reading of history may now castigate this ordering of society, yet at the time this was a way of dealing with the harsh realities of frontier life, a vortex of conflict among British Protestants, French Catholics, and Native Americans. It seems to me that both the English world of Wesley and the American world of Edwards experienced similar circumstances to Kenya's surreal destabilization by disease, poverty, and regional and global forces at the time that Oscar Muriu was on the rise. In these uncertain and precarious worlds, Edwards and other evangelists, such as George Whitefield, used unconventional means to lead people to experience the gospel afresh. Salvation came to be something that one could pursue, albeit with fear and trembling. The outcome was a series of mass conversions that came to be known as the Great Awakenings and the evangelical revival.

The leaders of the great revivals, "new lights" as they came to be known, were young antiestablishment preachers who used the expressive styles that were part of emerging popular theater culture but were hitherto unknown in church circles. Thus their preaching attracted thousands who had been alienated in existing churches. Whitefield, "the divine dramatist," for instance, addressed his sermons to the emotions of his hearers, adopting and transforming popular theatrical performances for sacred use with artfully staged humor, appeal to imagination, and extemporaneity.[13] The preaching of Whitefield and others like him had far-reaching effects, including attracting large numbers to the churches and meetings, to the extent that expressive preaching became a permanent, innovative feature of the developing movement (a century later Pentecostalism took this to the next level). In terms of church buildings, revivalist preachers generally

---

[12]George M. Marsden, *Jonathan Edwards: A Life* (New Haven: Yale University Press, 2003), 3-4.
[13]For instance, see Thomas S. Kidd, *George Whitefield: America's Spiritual Founding Father* (New Haven, CT: Yale University Press, 2014).

operated out of bare-minimum meetinghouses, buildings which, in contrast to ornate Anglican, Presbyterian, or Catholic architecture, were built to suit the essentialist community functions, beliefs, and activities of the Puritans.[14] It would be incumbent on the second-generation revivalists in the mid-nineteenth century to see that the logic of their revivalism required an ingathering of the numerous converts into worshiping communities (aha—the first "megachurches"!). Thus the nineteenth century was a time of great innovation with large structures to attract and retain crowds into revival meetings.[15] That second generation devised the sort of pragmatism that has been popular with evangelical icons such as Billy Graham during the second half of the twentieth century. They coordinated and publicized revival events as part of the developing evangelical movement. Newspaper editors loved these events because there was a ready market of spiritually awakened crowds in newly minted cities. Crowds morphed into congregations as energetic revivalist preachers—such as Charles Finney, Charles Spurgeon, D. L. Moody, and later Billy Sunday and Aimee Semple McPherson—recognized the spiritual thirst of the people who were settling into the modernizing city spaces for the very first time and built churches large enough to accommodate them.[16] During that generation the church building began to evolve through a variety of designs intended to hold large numbers.[17] This trend continued into the early twentieth century until the world wars and the Great Depression brought this sort of revivalism into recess.

---

[14]Anne C. Loveland and Otis B. Wheeler, *From Meetinghouse to Megachurch: A Material and Cultural History* (Columbia: University of Missouri Press, 2003).

[15]Loveland and Wheeler, *From Meetinghouse to Megachurch*, 16-17. They erected large temporary camp-meeting tents in the wilderness of frontier territories and in emerging cities, rented secular meeting halls and theaters, and eventually built movable tents, barns, warehouses, and tabernacles in poor neighborhoods to attract the poor, who did not go to high churches because they could not pay pew rentals or dress fashionably like the higher classes.

[16]See, for instance, Lyle W. Dorsett, *A Passion for Souls: The Life of D. L. Moody* (Chicago: Moody Publishers, 2003).

[17]Vaughan lists at least thirteen large congregations of the late nineteenth and early twentieth centuries. Chatham Street Chapel, a Presbyterian church in New York City led by Charles Finney, had enrolled 6,027 in Sunday school by 1889. Plymouth Church, led by Henry Beecher in Brooklyn, New York, had a regular attendance of 2,000 by 1860. Charles Spurgeon's Metropolitan Tabernacle in London had a capacity of 5,000 in 1861. D. L. Moody's Chicago Avenue Church had a capacity of up to 4,400 in 1894. See John N. Vaughan, *The World's Twenty Largest Churches* (Grand Rapids: Baker Books, 1984), 30-32.

In the second half of the twentieth century, the use of emotive preaching and large church buildings gained new synergy from an idea that emerged from the mission field: church-growth theory. Controversial as it is, church-growth theory remains best understood against the background of its missionary roots. While serving in India, Donald McGavran studied the churches under his supervision and found that, despite the numerous resources directed toward them, only 11 out of 147 churches were growing in any way. Looking into the causes, he discovered missionaries were trying to convert individuals in cultures where norms of social cohesion bound the communities tightly. In places where missionary churches were growing, people came to faith as whole people groups, *ethnes*. McGavran named these conversions "people movements." He challenged missionaries to fulfill the Great Commission by replacing evangelism of individuals with church plants that reach out to "homogenous units" of people in their social networks. This concept of church growth was revolutionary and unsettling to the old mission-station approach.[18]

Brought home from the mission field by returning missionaries, church-growth theory arrived in America just as its society was going through other changes that made the time ripe for such an idea. In the face of disenchantment with primary institutions of society—that is, government, church, and family—church attendance was waning. The practices of church-growth theory were proposed to help reawaken and repopulate the church. Baptist ministers such as Elmer Towns of First Baptist Church in Dallas and Jerry Falwell of Independent Baptist Church in Lynchburg, Virginia, were particularly effective in adapting church-growth theory to American entrepreneurial pragmatism. The "traditional church," they argued in writings, workshops, and seminars, was outdated for the later twentieth century. Average church services—the music, the titles, the dress, the language, the subjects discussed, the poor quality—isolated the average person, except those already convinced. These pastors called for a new type of church organization that would be relevant to contemporary American society and culture, the "innovative church."[19]

---

[18]See Donald McGavran, *Bridges of God: A Study in the Strategies of Mission* (Eugene, OR: Wipf and Stock, 2005).

[19]Loveland and Wheeler, *From Meetinghouse to Megachurch*, 117.

Church-growth theory also coincided with two other developments in broader American society. One was the idea from the business world that the "customer is king." To attract the unchurched, the innovative church must adopt a "marketing orientation" by defining a target audience through demographic and market research, then providing facilities to meet the needs of this customer. The second parallel development was the transformation in American urban design. All over the United States, the postwar years saw a boom in urban construction through the expansion of connecting roads and highways that allowed cities to expand into metropolises. This gave rise to the preeminence of the automobile as a mode of transportation. The American middle class, especially the white population, shifted away from city centers to newly developed suburbs.

Between the notion of customer as king and the expansion of highways and suburbs, church-growth theory came as a windfall to white American Christianity. A new generation of "community" and "regional" churches emerged in suburban outskirts. The advocates of church growth made converting the unchurched and the unsaved in large metropolises the raison d'être of this innovative church. Baby boomers, just then coming of age, were renamed "seekers" and offered "multiple services" and "quality ministries to the total man" in new church campuses.[20] These included therapeutic, educational, recreational, social, and community-service programs, libraries and bookstores, daycare facilities, Christian schools, sophisticated multimedia, and professional pageants. With more available land, suburban innovative churches could build huge campuses hosting entire complexes of buildings with ample parking. Many imitated the shopping malls of the mid- to late twentieth century, eschewing traditional structures, instead opting for themed buildings that would feel familiar, neutral, and comfortable for multiple experiences. They could also pay for largescale evangelism on radio, television, and newspapers; hire transport buses; and offer a wide range of services for various segments of the metropolitan population, such as counseling, Christian schools, and treatment and rehabilitation facilities.

And so these efforts bore fruit and the white, educated, middle-class American megachurches as we know them today came into being. An

---

[20]Loveland and Wheeler, *From Meetinghouse to Megachurch*, 189.

additional feature was the rise of Pentecostal and charismatic preachers who popularized an alternative brand of pragmatism by raising their personal profiles through broadcast television, radio, and later the internet. By emphasizing healing, addressing the material needs of those who remained in the lower stratum of society, and promoting the practice of "sowing seeds" for their ministries (to fund their expensive TV broadcasts) as part of their message, they acquired status as "global" preachers and expanded their reach beyond America.[21] They brought the idea of megachurches as large, glamorous, and affluent congregations into the living rooms of American homes and amplified the publicly visible, popular, conference-hopping pastor as an aspiration in the rest of the world. This remains the general image of the megachurch.

Over time this pragmatic expedience in response to changing urban and social dynamics has led to the critique that megachurches—by their efforts to reach the aspiring and middle-class demographic and their apparent display of the trappings of status, such as cars, large buildings, and use of technology—are captive to the entrepreneurial market. Because they have grown to be so big, megachurches are perceived to be largely concerned about numerical increase and attendant infrastructure. Since they employ contemporary technology and business organizational techniques, they "reify and reproduce ideologies related to the market and business." The conversational preaching styles, practical nature of sermons, humor, and high energy of the preachers, along with decor, drama, and use of popular culture are said to result in an impoverishing diet of "Christianity lite" that eschews a serious engagement with orthodox theology and traditional images, symbols, and rituals. The "commitment-phobic congregants" embrace a cheap theology of prosperity, the abundant life of good health, and deliverance from evil.[22] Add to this mix the sensational oddities of some megachurch pastors, the popularity of their self-help literature, the large annual leadership conferences, and other features that regularly place megachurch pastors on public pedestals. The scandals that haunt quite a

---

[21]For a detailed history of these types of churches, see Kate Bowler, *Blessed: A History of the American Prosperity Gospel* (New York: Oxford University Press, 2013).
[22]Virginia Garrard-Burnett, preface to *A Moving Faith: Mega Churches Go South*, ed. Jonathan D. James (Thousand Oaks, CA: Sage Publications, 2015), xi.

few of these churches tend to reflect poorly on all of them. The popularity of their music and televised broadcasts globally and the traffic gridlock their services cause locally render them suspect to the world, as such power dynamics are associated with inequality and scarcity on the one hand and divisive religion on the other. Meanwhile, to megachurch goers, the general disdain of outsiders does not distract from dazzling spectacle inside. Nearly all megachurches offer plenty of popular material that spans the range of hagiography, devotional writings, and leadership literature, as well as a variety of folksy ephemera to serve constituents and their networks. No wonder people ask if they have they sold out the soul of Christianity.

The resultant dislike of megachurches, especially the sharp censure of such large structures by the skeptical millennial generation in the West and around the world, is understandable. However, because of the inordinate attention that has been directed to these pragmatic aspects, critics have missed the fact that this type of Christianity has been seeking to interpret the sensibilities of the modernizing world—the city, the (capitalist) market, global realities, even modern politics—to a Christian demographic. Perhaps this is missed because it can only be seen in retrospect when considering megachurches with longer histories in dialogue with newer megachurches in freshly developing worlds.

Whether you go back to the Wesley brothers, Edwards, Whitefield, Finney, Spurgeon, Moody, Billy Sunday, Aimee Semple McPherson, Paul Yongi-Cho, David Oyedepo, Bill Hybels, Rick Warren, Sunday Adelaja, or any other persona that has historically attracted large followings or built megacongregations, these leaders and their followers come together at the intersection of generational transition and destabilizing social change. In such times, the leaders usually start out with the impulse to translate the gospel to a come-of-age generation that is not able to receive the gospel in the terms of earlier generations. For two hundred years, modernity has not made sense to most societies transitioning out of traditional worlds— neither in the West nor in the rest of the world. But the new megachurches appear to be making some sense of it, at least for their constituents. In their sermons about family, money, community, and politics, and in their social organization and use of technology, they are attempting a theological engagement that affirms what it means to live in the modern city, thrive in a capitalist world, and be globally connected, while also differentiating the Christian community from the world. Though many of them never quite accomplish this goal, it is their direction. It is because their activities make sense to a new generation, itself trying to make it in the modern world, that they end up attracting large numbers from that aspirational class. In effect, they "translate Christian truth, therefore transfer power, to a new generation."[23] In this, they empower new generations to find their place in the new world. They form what *New York Times* columnist David Brooks refers to as a "thick web of relationships" with new strong commitments to God and to one another as a countercultural community.[24] Many also have a cause, such as Mavuno's army of fearless influencers heading out to change the world. They articulate an inspiring mission statement that coalesces their attitude toward the world. They craft new group rituals (often embodied in music and reimagined liturgy or charismatic practices) that invite participation and new material symbols (such as use of social media or technology or community branding) that habituate belonging. All these are newly seen as the essence of flourishing. Never mind that much of this is experimental, fraught with internal leadership conflict (or struggles) and potential moral failure of leaders who, in many instances, "don't know what they are doing, they are learning on the go" (as in Nairobi Chapel in the 1990s) and are subject to the same crises as the congregants they lead. The key point is that it is attempted and does succeed in helping new generations make a cultural turn, which has the domino effect of inspiring change in the wider society as the gathered disperse to their workplaces after Sunday. Therefore, the rise of new megachurches around the world in the present historical moment—a moment of tangible transition into modernity for most Global-South nations—represents an opportune time to renew the conversation between Christianity and modernization, to reclaim the processes of modernization as a theological arena.

In a sense the big picture can only be seen in comparing those churches that have a longer historical experience and the newer ones because in the

---

[23]Mark Shaw, *Global Awakening: How 20th-Century Revivals Triggered a Christian Revolution* (Downers Grove, IL: IVP Academic, 2010), 16.

[24]David Brooks, *The Social Animal: The Hidden Sources of Love, Character, and Achievement* (New York: Random House, 2012), 23.

new churches there is a sense of possibility and aspiration toward greater achievements, and thus more pragmatic experimentation. It is this implication that has the most relevance to the conclusion I wish to draw from the story of Mavuno Church. That conclusion is not to tell the churches, mega or otherwise, how to refine their theology of Christianity and modernization—with a little sifting and sorting, that is all there in the contemporary pragmatism of megachurches. The conclusion has to do with the basic pattern of the translation process. Although Mavuno has done and continues to do well for its twelve-year timeline, historical hindsight into two hundred years of evangelical pragmatism—and the megachurches that have grown and faded through the seasons—provides a cautionary tale. The devil is in the details, no pun intended. Leaders energetically begin the task of translating the gospel to a new generation, but as soon as they attract a large crowd that becomes a community, they often fail to move the community on to full maturity. Perhaps this is because the community and the movements that emerge remain centered on leaders who are singularly gifted, or perhaps they are not able to develop new wineskins that allow for more use of the gifts of the body of Christ.

Therefore, the caution I see is the inability to complete the task of translating the gospel. First, the leadership must understand the volatility holding a society back, as well as the transitional chokepoints of a generation (see chapter two). The church then has to locate the essentials of Christian discipleship in their rightful place, as the Mavuno Marathon attempts to do (see chapter three), develop the appropriate wineskins of leadership in context (see chapter four), and lead the new generation to reclaim their personal and cultural identity (see chapter five). Each stage calls for recognizing varying degrees of connection, maturity, and missional engagement within the community of faith, both local and universal. The Mavuno Marathon, therefore, though designed for the Kenyan and African millennial demographic, gives us a sample outline of the process. On the one end are people who are indifferent, who either have no contact with the gospel or have elected to be indifferent because they cannot see its relevance to real life. Mavuno Church calls them "complacent." On the other end are those who are integrally connected in the church community, totally sold out to the gospel and empowered to serve the mission of God in the world. Mavuno calls them "compelled." In between are people at varying stages of relationship with God and some degree of connection to church life and its community. Mavuno calls these "consumers," "connected," and "committed." Once the essential pattern is understood, a good deal of the actual process of transferring the power of the gospel from the old to the new generation turns on language and communication, so that one could easily replace traditional Christianese with the words Mavuno Church uses or with postmodern phraseologies, as does much of the literature from the emerging-church movement. What is critical is to understand the changed parameters of the social worlds, how the gospel has become unintelligible to them, and how it can be made clear and transformational again. This is what megachurches attempt to do and their mountain of internal leadership and ephemeral literature addresses the disparate aspects of this proposal.[25]

Yet what I want to do here is to underscore the cultural process of getting people out of complacent society, through the stages of consumer, connected, and committed, and finally to compelled followers of Jesus Christ. It is not a new task. Looking again into Christian history, we recognize it as the same crosscultural process that the gospel has followed throughout its two thousand years of passing from one culture to the next, from one generation to the other. Missionary scholars have been pointing out for decades that there is no way we can engage with the gospel independent of culture, because our interaction with the gospel relies on human language, worldviews, and lived realities.[26] Churches in non-Western contexts know how closely the gospel is wedded to culture, but it has been a rude awakening for the church in the West to come to terms with its own cultural weddedness, particularly through recent political events. So the recovery of the Christian cultural imperative is not just for megachurches or the church in the majority world. It is an essential task for all Christian communities. A basic theological understanding of how the gospel penetrates across cultures is required (however culture is conceived, whether

---

[25]For extensive resources that can help with this goal, see Warren Bird's Leadership Network website: http://leadnet.org/.
[26]See the introductory essay in Harold A. Netland and Craig Ott, eds., *Globalizing Theology: Belief and Practice in an Era of World Christianity* (Grand Rapids: Baker Academic, 2006).

from settings that are rural or urban, traditional or modern, monocultural or multicultural, having singular or pluralistic worldviews, or possessing an eclectic mix of influences). This task of translating from one generation to the next across changed cultural realities is often complicated by method and structure. But the process is quite simple, as has been demonstrated over the last century as Christianity has been transmitted to "raw cultures" across the Global South. I will expound on this idea in the conclusion.

Conclusion

The Cultural-Translation Process

RELATIVIZATION VERSUS REVITALIZATION

Scholars and historians of world Christianity, such as Lamin Sanneh, Andrew Walls, and Kwame Bediako, studying the crosscultural patterns of how Christianity was translated from its European phase to its phase around the world over the course of the twentieth century, came to a startling conclusion. As Christianity passes into a new culture, it is initially *relativized* by the new culture, but it eventually *revitalizes* it.[1] This is the effect of a successful translation process. The same dynamic is to be observed of megachurches as they attempt to pass Christianity from an older, acculturated generation to a generation whose cultural realities have changed through modernization.

Christianity makes a way, takes root, and thrives in a culture because of the initial act of Christ's incarnation as a human. God in the person of Jesus became incarnate in the Jewish world. The local Jewish idiom was and remains the chosen cultural vessel of the bodily incarnation of Jesus for translating the divine message of salvation into human language through

---

[1]This is in fact the sum of much of their writing, to explain the crosscultural transmission of the Christian faith into the raw cultures of Africa that had not had an encounter with the gospel before the missionary era. See Lamin O. Sanneh, *Translating the Message: The Missionary Impact on Culture,* American Society of Missiology Series 13 (Maryknoll, NY: Orbis Books, 1989); Kwame Bediako, *Jesus in Africa: The Christian Gospel in African History and Experience,* Theology in Africa Series (Maryknoll, NY: Orbis Books, 2004); Andrew Walls, *The Cross-Cultural Process in Christian History: Studies in the Transmission and Appropriation of Faith* (Maryknoll, NY: Orbis Books, 2002).

the historical experience of Israel and the church in New Testament. Since its foundations, Christianity has been inextricably wedded to culture and follows the same patterns of translation to successive generations among human societies, both linguistically and culturally. Christianity therefore possesses the strength of "infinite cultural translatability." However, this infinite translatability introduces into the gospel both its fragility and strength, "embedded in the very founding documents of the faith."[2] The fragility is that, as the gospel makes entry into a new culture, it is *relativized* by the culture; the strength is that as the gospel makes a home in the culture, it *revitalizes*, that is, strengthens, that culture. Andrew Walls frames this as two paradoxical tendencies. He calls them the indigenizing principle and the pilgrim principle.

On the one hand, the gospel is the good news that God invites and accepts people wherever they are in their culture on the ground of Christ's work alone, not based on what they already are. The indigenizing principle associates Christians with the *particulars* of their culture. For Christianity to make a home in any culture, it must always make an initial critical interface with the cultural materials of the given era. The crossing point has never been painless, and the tension or pain of cultural translation is what comes across as a *relativizing* influence on the gospel as previously experienced in a different culture. Today Christians like to use the words "no one is perfect" to explain the fragility of being Christian but not living the ideal of the golden rule or the Sermon on the Mount, for instance. Oddly, many fail to connect the fragility of an individual's faith to the similar fragility of a community or culture in the early stages of learning to embrace the faith. Just as an individual must struggle to learn to be a Christian, so Christianity makes its way into any new cultural group in imperfect ways, depending on the religious and social background conditions, through the slow and patient work of the Spirit of God. This makes it seem as if the gospel is being diluted. It is counterintuitive to imagine the gospel relativized by culture, but the option of not engaging with culture leads to, as Sanneh observes, a Christianity that is either opposed to culture or is culturally bound—one that dominates through fundamentalism or

---

[2]Andrew F. Walls, *The Missionary Movement in Christian History: Studies in the Transmission of Faith* (Maryknoll, NY: Orbis, 1996), 22.

one that is co-opted through liberalism. And we know how this has resulted in culture wars in the North American church.[3] The ideal is where a mature church provides a prophetic witness to the world, where Christians find that balance of being in the world but not of it. But arriving here takes a dialogue with culture in which relativization is inevitable. So, yes, there is a legitimate concern about "Christianity lite" in new megachurches. Pastors who sense that they must make the gospel "relevant" risk leaning too closely into elements of culture that seem to be far away from what we think of as standard theology.

On the other hand, once a group of Christ's followers from a cultural setting has sensed God's divine acceptance, a second movement in the translation process begins to take place, which Walls calls the "pilgrim principle."[4] The gospel at once reaches people *in* their culture and then leads them on a journey *away from* their culture as a community of faith, which joins the universal body of Christ. Thus, to follow Christ is to eventually get out of step with one's culture, because there is no culture that can wholly absorb the Word of God. As a new community's cultural norms are transformed by the values of the gospel, the gospel *revitalizes* that community. Then, if the community has a salt and light effect in its wider world, it goes on to revitalize the culture. The indigenizing principle allows pastors to find resources within a culture to communicate the gospel. The pilgrim principle calls converts to learn not only from Scripture but also from materials that are not available in their own culture, including resources from the universal body of Christ and the communion of saints throughout history. As the word *pilgrim* implies, this transformation is not a quick event; the difference between the indigenous and the pilgrim principles is *time* and *process*. This is seen, for instance, in the Mavuno

---

[3]A Christianity that is opposed to culture practices stringent spirituality where faithful believers quarantine themselves, maintaining a close vigilance over their life in relative seclusion from the rest of the world. They believe they have made a break with the unrighteous world. This may sound all right, but the quarantine becomes permanent and creates extreme marginalization of the Christian community. This sort of Christianity becomes irrelevant to the world and eventually leads to secularization of the rest of society because it has given up on being salt and light. See Lamin Sanneh, *Encountering the West: Christianity and the Global Cultural Process, the African Dimension*, World Christian Theology Series (Maryknoll, NY: Orbis Books, 1993), 16; see also James Davison Hunter, *To Change the World: The Irony, Tragedy, and Possibility of Christianity in the Late Modern World* (New York: Oxford University Press, 2010).
[4]Walls, *Missionary Movement*, 8-9.

Marathon, which shows that Christian maturity is a continuum that occurs over time through the human developmental seasons and only effectively through generational cross-influence. Let me illustrate this with two examples of the translation process and transfer of power from the twentieth century that are well known to scholars of world Christianity.

Two Paradigmatic Examples of Translation in the Twentieth Century

AIC Christianity in contrast to missionary Christianity in India. Vernacular translation was the tour de force of Christianity's growth in twentieth-century Africa. Right from the start, Protestant missions made literacy and translation of the Bible the centerpiece of their mission work. Missionaries believed the content of the Bible wholeheartedly and believed that if Africans could read the Bible for themselves, they would embrace Christianity the way the missionaries did. Although missionaries had less success in the way of converts, their efforts at Bible translation proved successful beyond their wildest dreams. Scripture was often the first literature to appear in an African language.[5] But one flaw was that the missionaries did not see the continuity between the biblical world and the African worlds. They tried to make European Christians out of Africans. Once the Bible was translated into vernaculars, Africans were quick to realize it lent more support to their traditional African customs than to the imported cultural customs of European missionaries. The discovery of the continuities between the African worlds and the biblical worlds was astonishing. Biblical stories affirmed such realities as kinship networks, structures of social organization and rites of passage, and manifestations of evil in the world, even denouncing oppression under the colonial settler, among others. African practices of maintaining social order—such as honoring ancestors and elders, atonement performances, and using certain means of instructing children and young people—were part and parcel of biblical narratives. The Bible, Africans came to realize, was allied to their view of a world in which community was central, life was enchanted by good and evil, and the living were in an active relationship with the

---

[5]Sanneh, *Translating the Message*, 105-25.

supernatural world. Because of these different readings, breakaways from missionary churches, known as African Indigenous Churches (AICs), begun to occur early in the missionary era.[6] AICs incorporated many aspects of African culture that missionaries had not embraced. Missionaries did not expect this to happen, but Africans did not see themselves as breaking away from the true gospel; they were embracing their cultures as reflected in biblical stories. This stumped the missionaries, who called these churches sectarian, syncretistic, and schismatic in relation to their own type of Christianity.[7] In actual fact, AICs never matured into sublime evangelical or orthodox Christian theology, but the *cultural turn* of AIC Christianity accounts for the difference between an African continent that currently has 450 million Christians and an Indian subcontinent that has only 60 million Christians.

Though, as scholars tell us, more missionary resources were sent to India than to Africa in the eighteenth and nineteenth centuries, today Africa has more Christian converts than India, although both continents house over a billion people.[8] Why? Because the Christianity that missionaries planted in India was largely seen to be foreign and linked to colonialism. In the historical conditions of colonial struggle, the attempts to indigenize Indian Christianity were met with great resistance and were unsuccessful. Indian Christians never developed a worldview that engaged traditional Indian deities and social customs.[9] On the other hand, historical conditions in

---

[6]See one of the leading writings on this: Allan Anderson, *African Reformation: African Initiated Christianity in the 20th Century* (Trenton, NJ: Africa World Press, 2001).

[7]Adrian Hastings is correct in noting that most of the schisms that produced the AIC churches were no different from the patterns of Anglo-Saxon Protestantism, for whom the theoretical Protestant appeal to the Bible was an inherent ground for division. The missionaries had carried their seed to Africa only too faithfully. Despite the primary distinctives of evangelicalism, variety of expression was common long before it came to Africa. Though the movement was a recognizable one, it was also in several respects diverse—in theology, denomination, social characteristics, and geographical location. Africans saw themselves reproducing the exact same thing. Adrian Hastings, *The Church in Africa: 1450-1950*, Oxford History of the Christian Church (New York: Oxford University Press, 2004), 498-99.

[8]See Walls, *Cross-Cultural Process*.

[9]Frykenberg writes that one of the most lingering, persistent, and stubborn misconceptions both in India and in the West is the notion that Christianity is essentially European and that European religion has traditionally been Christianity. The real story is far more complex as it needs to account for St. Thomas Christianity, which dates back to the first century, as well as the early Jesuits; still, the perception of foreignness endures. Robert Eric Frykenberg and Alaine M. Low, *Christians and Missionaries in India: Cross-Cultural Communication Since 1500*, with

Africa did not stop the indigenous movements; instead the new religious movements became variously allied to colonial struggle. This translation act was necessary to the historical development of the Christian movement in Africa. Through cultural practices and political alliances, AICs indigenized, and to some degree enculturated and contextualized, Christianity for a world that was then transitioning from the isolation of primordial realities to the intrusion of external global forces. A similar comparison can be made between Korean Christianity, where Christianity became allied with the goals of nationhood, and Christianity in Japan or China, where over the same period of time Christianity entered into a conflictual relationship with nationalist quests, thus failing to indigenize at a crucial phase of modern state construction.

For Africa this indigenization provided the initial theological bedrock for the gospel to wrestle with traditional realities of the African world, such as polygamy or chieftaincy, names of God, idioms, proverbs, stories, and everything that could be expressed via vernacular means, initially through linguistic translation and eventually through cultural translation. As Sanneh has noted, this unique encounter with Africa renewed Christianity's ability to negotiate with cultures in a way it has not done in any other continent. Christianity itself has been affected, "relativized," in the form of all those so-called "syncretistic" churches and practices.[10] Yet insofar as Christianity has successfully penetrated African societies, this is largely because it has been assimilated into the local idiom and cultures. AICs did not even resolve cultural questions, but simply adopting whatever practices they did raised their relevance for ecclesiastical rejoinders and future theological conversations. For instance, when combative nationalists and literary writers made a Janus-faced about turn on Christianity in the immediate postcolonial moment, the questions and issues raised by AICs provided the basis for conversation among African theologians in the 1960s and 1970s.[11]

Special Reference to Caste, Conversion, and Colonialism (Grand Rapids: Eerdmans, 2003); see also the chapter on the Dornakal Revival, the encounter between Mahatma Gandhi and Bishop V. S. Azariah, in Mark Shaw, *Global Awakening: How 20th-Century Revivals Triggered a Christian Revolution* (Downers Grove, IL: IVP Academic, 2010), 67-90.

[10]Sanneh, *Encountering the West*, 16.

[11]See the previews of those conversations in Diane B. Stinton, *Jesus of Africa: Voices of Contemporary African Christology*, Faith and Cultures Series (Maryknoll, NY: Orbis Books, 2004).

Within the ecclesial sphere, AIC Christianity triggered the reactive response of other renewal movements, such as the East African Revival, Aliliki in Zimbabwe, and Christ Apostolic Church in Nigeria in the 1930s and 1940s. These evangelical reactions were countermeasures to correct what they saw as the adulteration of the gospel by both the nominal missionary Christianity and the deviant AIC movements. It is well known that these more evangelical revival movements renewed mainline churches with an evangelical gospel well into the 1970s. When the vitality of the likes of the East Africa Revival faded, the neo-Pentecostal churches, such as Deliverance Church in Kenya, Redeemed Christian Church of God, Winners Chapel in Nigeria, and Light-House International in Ghana, arose to preach what they called a "full gospel." These same churches later developed a strong Christian subculture that was incomprehensible to the next generation, the millennials. The neo-Pentecostals nevertheless had a grip on reality in the otherwise surreal world of poverty and political upheaval in the 1980s and 1990s; similarly, the megachurches of the new generation—Nairobi Chapel and others, such as the Nairobi Pentecostal Churches in Kenya, Watoto Church in Uganda, and Celebrate Ministries International in Zimbabwe, among others. Although these churches do not share direct histories, and while many define themselves over against the older forms, they are not discontinuous to those who came before them. They can only build because those earlier Christianities tilled the cultural soil and planted the seed in response to the issues in their own times—the act of translating the power of the gospel to a generation. We need to recover the perspective that this relativization, which is precipitated by the volatile changes in society, goes hand in hand with revitalization, which is the result of a new faith community bringing a prophetic witness to society after the awakening of a generation.

South Korean Christianity's successful negotiation of modernization. A second example to demonstrate the indigenizing and pilgrim principles comes from Christianity in South Korea. While AICs point to the essential task of breaking primal ground between Christianity and traditional religion, Korean Christianity suggests how translation can occur in the midst of modernizing social change, again over the course of at least two or three generations of Christian presence.

In sociological studies, Korea is seen as the poster child of globalization, a cultural chessboard on which forces of capitalism, communism, indigenous religion, and Western Christianity have clashed.[12] Despite all the external powers that vied for its territory throughout the twentieth century, South Korea has come into its own as a modernized nation. Korean Christianity has also successfully navigated and transitioned through the old worlds and overwhelming global odds into a self-consciously indigenous yet modern faith with a thriving missionary movement. South Korea is also home both to large and smaller megachurches, plus small community churches of the similar ethos, which exhibit a great deal of ecclesial maturity in their discipleship and missional commitments. They offer a possible direction for megachurches from other parts of the Global South to consider too.[13]

How has this indigenization occurred alongside modernization? Christianity first came to Korea in the seventeenth and eighteenth centuries via Chinese Christian literature imported by Korean scholars, but for a time it was seen as a foreign religion. After 1884 there was an influx of Presbyterian and Methodist missionaries who built schools, hospitals, and churches. Just as in Africa, they translated the Bible into the language of the common people, in this case Hangul. In 1895, after the Sino-Japanese treaty, Korea began to enter the world of modern nation-states. However, in another spate of geopolitical struggles between regional and global powers, Japan annexed Korea in 1910, which began another era of instability in the Korean peninsula. Between 1903 and 1907, as political forces were wreaking havoc on the national psyche, a Christian revival took place in Wonsan, Seoul, and Pyongyang. For the badly demoralized Korean people, the revival led to exploration of spiritual solutions—intensified prayer in the mountains, pursuit of holiness, and church growth—to Korea's cultural crisis of humiliation at the hands of the Japanese for thirty-six years. Koreans looked to church-based renewal to make sense of the national crisis.

After the world wars and Korea's liberation from Japan, a concept of nationalism developed that required spiritual renewal as a necessary

---

[12]Shaw, *Global Awakening*, 35-36.
[13]Kim Jinbong, P. Dwight Baker, and J. Nelson Jennings, eds., *Megachurch Accountability in Missions: Critical Assessment Through Global Case Studies* (Pasadena, CA: William Carey Library, 2016). See especially the chapters by Chang Ju Kim, "Korean Megachurches in Mission," and Pil-Hun Park, "Megachurch Mission Agency Interaction: A Case Study of SaRang Church."

precondition. As Korean politicians poured energy into building a modern nation centered on self-reliance, Christian leaders urged the church to play a part through a visible Christian nationalism shaped by spiritual restoration, moral reformation, and purposeful action.[14] A message of prosperity on a continuum of ethical lifestyle and work discipline, pious devotion, and dependence on the miraculous accompanied this Christian nationalism. As a result of the Korean War of 1950–1953, Korea underwent another period of cultural humiliation through its division into North and South during the cold war. Again Korean Christians allied the ambitions of their nationalist leaders to solutions in the spiritual realm. A new wave of revivals led by Pentecostal, Presbyterian, and Methodist pastors encouraged congregants to back government policies that were designed to build a strong economy, because they saw economic development as essential to preserving Korean independence over against intrusive global forces, particularly communism.[15] The famously large megachurches grew out of this indigenized Christianity. This new generation of revivals continued the previous ethos of nationalistic spirituality and also took the traditional shamanistic worldview seriously. They reinterpreted and redefined traditional animism as ecstatic gifts of the Holy Spirit and the presence of good and evil in the world. They translated the realities of heaven and hell into new understandings of material blessing, and practices of kinship and family into piety, humility, and repentance in church community. Over the course of the second half of the twentieth century, this shamanistic interface with Pentecostalism, which was also absorbed by mainline churches, allowed Korean Christians to incorporate their nation's rapidly modernizing outlook with their Christian identity.

Thus, it is not surprising that Korean Christianity did not divorce modernization from Christianity and that part of that success was an unprecedented growth of churches of all kinds. Despite flattening generalizations that characterize them as Pentecostal and charismatic, Korea's megachurches and other smaller but thriving churches have a broad range of

[14]Shaw, *Global Awakening*, 42.
[15]Kirsteen Kim, "Ethereal Christianity: Reading Korean Mega-Church Websites," *Studies in World Christianity* 13, no. 3 (December 1, 2007): 208-24.

denominational representation. There are traditional churches that em-
phasize orthodox doctrines of evangelical pietism and conservative faith.
There are middle-class-style churches that tend toward an intellectual and
spiritual emphasis on Scripture, drawing largely from the Gospels and the
early chapters of Acts. A third style emphasizes religious experience, the
presence of the Holy Spirit, prayer, and evangelism.[16] The common denom-
inator is indigeneity—a sense of ownership and alignment of spirituality
with the general goals of the individual, a strong community, and national
prosperity. Korea became a special enclave of Christianity in East Asia and
the leading home of megachurches because church leaders forged a creative
engagement between the nation's need for a spirit of nationalism with the
appropriate work ethic and the message of the gospel. This Christianity,
while pious and deeply missional, is definitely not "other-worldly."[17] The
average churchgoer believes that by embracing Christianity, he or she will
gain plenty of material success in this world and spiritual rewards in the
next. While the Korean church may need to turn another corner to reach
its millennial generation, this twentieth-century adaptation is an example
of a successful translation process in the modernizing world, particularly
for churches rising in other modernizing parts of the world like Africa.

Toward a Fully Realized Translation Process

Here is where the rubber meets the road for the study of a church that
has grown to mega size. Megachurch Christianity all over the world, even
in its older American forms, sits in the niche where the AICs and their
descendants once sat, the niche of popular Christianity that produces a
grassroots theology for local communities experiencing externally insti-
gated change. The earlier AICs addressed matters that were significant at
that time. Now megachurches are on the frontline of making sense of—
translating—the cultural realities of modernity as it is experienced as a
new social force.[18] In this way megachurches have been renewing the

---

[16]Hong Young-Gi, "The Backgrounds and Characteristics of the Charismatic Mega-Churches
in Korea," *Asia Journal of Pentecostal Studies* 3, no. 1 (2000): 102-3.

[17]Young Gi Hong, "The Impact of Charismatic Pastoral Leadership on Religious Commitment
and Church Growth in the Korean Mega-Churches," *Mission Studies* 18, no. 2036 (2001).

[18]See Steve Offutt's study of what he calls new centers of evangelicalism. These places across
the Global South that are becoming socioeconomically independent, internationally connected,

significance of religion—Christianity—as a social force in human affairs that matter, such as economics, politics, and the expansion of cities, a renewal that is necessary because of the post-Enlightenment banishment of Christianity from public space. They need to engage in a fully realized translation process so that they can resource the spheres created by modernity—economic arrangements, education, law and government, arts, entertainment, business, and science as they are experienced in nations coming into their own—with a holistic, Christian-informed ethical vision.

As discussed in chapter six, despite its longer existence in older nations, the Western evangelical church has not provided such a script because it has been odds with these very aspects of modernity. Now it is especially urgent because all of Christianity evolving across the Global South has to do so alongside these other social processes. The megachurches are pulled between indigenous cultural impulses and pilgrim impulses where the new community forms part of the body of Christ, local and universal, contemporary and historical. The indigenous impulse means they can be expected to have plenty of preexisting cultural blinkers. If, as Walls puts it, we can only receive new ideas in terms of ideas we already have, then the elements of modern secular culture—such as consumer-driven capitalism with its advertising, marketing, and adaptive communication technologies—are the initial places where the gospel is meeting with cultural reality. This is where startup megachurches are found. As the gospel interacts with a modernizing culture, the ideas of both the gospel and modernity will be expanded. Leading people on this path holds the intrinsic tension between relativizing the gospel, as, for instance, they are entertained as consumers in a church service, and revitalizing the church and culture, as they become dedicated followers of Christ and compelled fearless influencers of society.

Some Christians would like to think they are not of this world, and so turn their backs on conversations that engage with concepts of modernity. Yet there is no way to circumvent the messiness of modernity apart from

and socially engaged, evangelical leaders and entrepreneurs are busily building socially engaged organizations. He argues that these are recreating evangelical identity, but I would argue that they are in fact confirming its enduring character. Stephen Offutt, *New Centers of Global Evangelicalism in Latin America and Africa* (Cambridge: Cambridge University Press, 2015); see also Robert Wuthnow, *Boundless Faith: The Global Outreach of American Churches* (Berkeley: University of California Press, 2009).

engaging it. Look at the content of megachurch preaching anywhere today: it uses today's idioms, whether economic, linguistic, musical, or techno-logical. It applies the gospel directly to the experience of daily life and largely remains at odds with traditional theology that is focused on other-worldly reality (the sharp secular/sacred divide). These communities thrive on strong ties of belonging within newly forged aspiring middle-class networks. Feelings are strongly expressed through experiential worship and contemporary artsy forms, albeit imported ones. These are the markers of what anthropologists call folk or popular religion.[19] Megachurches also grow in a world in which human agency—active, willful, goal-seeking action—is central to how religious life takes place. Each action is deliber-ately chosen, planned, executed, and evaluated. Scholars who have been observing contemporary megachurches, such as Paul Gifford in his books on Kenyan and Ghanaian Christianities, write much about this practical instrumentality that drives popular religion.[20] The insistence on faith healing and material success and the elevation of symbolic or literal materiality, such as big churches, large media ministries, international expansion, in-stitutions of higher education, themes of conferences, music, testimonies, and literature, echo deeply felt needs and conscious opting for what matters *now*.[21] It is said that megachurches do not address the issue of suffering. However, their existence is an antithesis to the social volatility out of which they emerge in the first place. Personal dysfunctions—ranging from material deprivation to substance dependence, broken marriages, depression, and social exclusion—are part and parcel of the dark side of modernity. Their impact as agents of individual and family misery, relative to social location, are not to be underestimated. This broad matrix of personal pain is why congregants welcome fervent church life; upbeat, energetic, or otherwise deeply resonant music; and sermons and literature on miracles, positive

---

[19]Paul G. Hiebert, *Understanding Folk Religion: A Christian Response to Popular Beliefs and Practices* (Grand Rapids: Baker Academic, 2000).

[20]Paul Gifford, *Ghana's New Christianity: Pentecostalism in a Globalising African Economy* (London: Hurst & Co, 2004); Gifford, *Christianity, Politics and Public Life in Kenya* (New York: Columbia University Press, 2009).

[21]See J. Kwabena Asamoah-Gyadu, "Doing Greater Things: Mega Church as an African Phe-nomenon," in *A Moving Faith: Mega Churches Go South*, ed. Jonathan D. James (Thousand Oaks, CA: Sage Publications, 2015).

thinking, pursuit of purpose or meaning, and success as a source of renewal, hope, and eventually breakthrough.

Although only some churches have made peace with it, these are the conditions in which the new phase of the expansion of Christianity is taking root. If Walls, Sanneh, and others are right about the principle of translation as the tension between two realities, then this is as it should be, with the indigenizing principle at work as the gospel interfaces with a cultural reality that is otherwise distant from matters of faith. Rather than being at odds with the materiality of the modern world, new Christianities are seeking to expand the language of Christianity to be congruent with the present context. For instance, prosperity-oriented preaching, although not fully developed in most cases, is trying to expand the language of the gospel and the language of capitalism to make them congruent with the life of the modern person, while accommodating an audience that wants to be both capitalist and Christian. Similar accommodations are evident with the influence of cultural globalization through information technology, music, literature, movies, and social media. These are warp and woof of modern life, and aspirational megachurch goers are back in church because they want to embrace the gospel *and* be successful at work, at home, and in their social lives. After all, that's why they got an education.

Andrew Walls insists that translation uses the terms and relations of specific historical contexts, just as the original translation of the Son of God was in Jewish context "under Pontius Pilate." The use of media, the construction of mall-like churches in suburbs, and even success in material wealth constitutes the historical context of the twenty-first century. Materiality does not have to be antithetical to the gospel insofar as it is an inevitable social dynamic in which Christianity is seeking to make a home with a new generation. Pursuit of success, health, security, and an abundant life, however conceived, is the goal of progress in the modern world—why should it be a surprise that anyone going to church is also pursuing a successful life in a way displays that success? Learning to better manage organizations, both businesses and nonprofits, is one of the great achievements of the twentieth century—why is it a problem if churches study best business practices and organize their congregants, resources, and missional goals better, using market ideas? Cities have attracted and grown to accommodate millions of people. They have built stadiums that seat hundreds of thousands of people for entertainment purposes. Why is it a surprise that such cities of millions attract a few thousand to a single church? Instead of arguing about the dimensions of the "narrow gate" (Mt 7:13), should we not be attempting to get as many as possible of the millions in our cities back to church?

Just like the AICs and older Pentecostals, megachurch Christianity is producing a frontier grassroots theology by bridging contemporary cultural realities and the message of the gospel. Granted, just as with the initial crosscultural encounters, the current frontier produces a grassroots theology that is potentially borderline syncretistic, which may otherwise come across as "Christianity lite," or as Os Guinness calls it, a Christianity of "cheap grace."[22] Extrapolating from the American context, Guinness writes that modern megachurches have been built on the philosophical and structural pattern of America's shopping malls, "cathedrals of consumption." The darker side of this innovative genius, he argues, is the temptation to compromise with worldly markers of success and size, the dependence on the amplifying power of technology, and the replacement of faith and God's authority with methods.[23] Touché. What Guinness is gesturing toward is Andrew Walls's caution that if churches indigenize but never grow into mature Christian communities that identify more with the universal body of Christ than with their culture, they end up being "culture churches" in which "no one else can find a home"—the problem of "cultural captivity," as Sanneh puts it. "Blood is thicker than water," we say in African lore. Or as savvy observers of megachurches with longer histories point out, the fictive kinship within these churches does turn inward, where numerical and material success is seen to be self-validating, while stability and predictability within render them tone deaf to broader socioeconomic concerns.[24]

---

[22]Os Guinness, *Dining with the Devil: The Megachurch Movement Flirts with Modernity* (Grand Rapids: Baker Books, 1993), 58.

[23]Guinness, *Dining with the Devil*, 36.

[24]In the American context from which Guinness's book is written, a variety of perspectives on this cultural captivity may be found in these recent works: Robert Wuthnow, *After the Baby Boomers: How Twenty- and Thirty-Somethings Are Shaping the Future of American Religion* (Princeton: Princeton University Press, 2007); Thomas Bergler, *The Juvenilization of American*

Yet the answer to the problem of cheap-grace Christianity or cultural captivity is not in embracing more esoteric novelty, either in language or worship practices. This is because, as Eugene Peterson puts it, life is lived in the routine trenches of everydayness, and agency in the world is mediated through the mundane rhythms of living.[25] People want to know how to practice faith in a human body in which all the senses are alive, not spirituality abstracted in the brain. Christlike character is an outworking of discipleship in the ordinariness of working, loving, and playing.[26] A faith forged through esoteric novelty may cater to a select few, but most people remain in the mainstream of culture. That doesn't mean they are opposed to the values of the gospel; they seek a model of faith that makes sense within those regular rhythms. So many in the newly aspirational class flock to megachurches because something about what they convey, however inadequate, is amenable to urban everydayness. This is also why megachurches themselves need to gain greater clarity on the full translation process without losing the detail that makes each one culturally unique.

Once clarity has been gained, there is nothing to it: a mountain of ordinary literature on spiritual formation, catechisms, adult education, and so on speaks to this quest to lead people to increasing levels of maturity in the faith, where kin, cultural, generational, and ethnic identities are transcended by a communal identity established by spiritual bonds of discipleship to Christ and belonging in the universal body of Christ—that is, an identity marked by the cross. The particularities of church polity and practices, worship and liturgy, education and community formation, prophetic witness, and missionary work are cultural matters left up to the leadership. As we can discern from the experience of Oscar Muriu and Muriithi Wanjau, the critical call of leadership at any one time depends on the positioning of the actors, the present needs of the local people, the institutional resources available, and the perceived trajectories into the future. The successful translation of the gospel to new generations lies with

Christianity (Grand Rapids: Eerdmans, 2012); Christian Smith and Michael O. Emerson, American Evangelicalism: Embattled and Thriving (Chicago: University of Chicago Press, 1998).
[25] Eugene H. Peterson, Leap over a Wall: Earthy Spirituality for Everyday Christians (San Francisco, CA: HarperSanFrancisco, 1997).
[26] Mark R. Shaw, Work, Play, Love: A Visual Guide to Calling, Career and the Mission of God (Downers Grove, IL: InterVarsity Press, 2014).

churches of whatever size or polity that uphold the intrinsic tension between the indigenizing impulse, which finds people wherever they are, and the pilgrim impulse, which leads people on a realistic journey toward the New Jerusalem. Megachurches are not the only form of church that facilitates the translation process. There is a significant movement toward small church communities, especially in societies that have a generational perspective on the shortcomings of large churches. It is the ethos of what they do, their pragmatism in engaging modernizing processes in obedience to the Great Commission, that will provide a script for renewed dialogue with the patterns of culture in their twenty-first-century forms.

There are two additional advantages that contemporary megachurch Christianity has over earlier AICs and Pentecostal churches. First, the self-conscious and conscientious actions of leaders like Muriithi Wanjau means that while megachurches seek to scratch the world where it itches, so to speak, historical precedents oblige them to build communities that demonstrate a level of maturity that their forerunners only saw through a glass darkly. This is especially true because, second, contemporary mega-churches can marshal substantial institutional and financial resources, network, learn, and avoid the mistakes of their forebears. This catapults today's megachurches into their own sphere of the mainstream, where they must continue to adapt their prophetic witness in worlds that will continue to be destabilized by rapid change.

Further Reading

ACM-FTT Afriserve. *The Unfinished Task: A National Survey of Churches in Kenya.* Nairobi: ACM-FTT Afriserve, in partnership with Dawn Ministries, 2004.

African Development Bank. "The Middle of the Pyramid: Dynamics of the Middle Class in Africa." *Market Brief.* April 20, 2011. www.afdb.org/fileadmin /uploads/afdb/Documents/Publications/The%20Middle%20of%20the%20 Pyramid_The%20Middle%20of%20the%20Pyramid.pdf.

Anderson, Allan. *African Reformation: African Initiated Christianity in the 20th Century.* Trenton, NJ: Africa World Press, 2001.

Anderson, David. *Histories of the Hanged: Britain's Dirty War in Kenya and the End of Empire.* New York: Norton, 2011.

Arnett, Jeffrey Jensen. *Emerging Adulthood: The Winding Road from the Late Teens Through the Twenties.* New York: Oxford University Press, 2004.

Asamoah-Gyadu, J. Kwabena. *Contemporary Pentecostal Christianity: Interpretations from an African Context.* Eugene, OR: Wipf & Stock, 2013.

Bediako, Kwame. *Jesus and the Gospel in Africa: History and Experience.* Maryknoll, NY: Orbis Books, 2004.

———. *Jesus in Africa: The Christian Gospel in African History and Experience.* Theology in Africa. Maryknoll, NY: Orbis Books, 2004.

Berger, Peter L. *The Sacred Canopy: Elements of a Sociological Theory of Religion.* Reprint, New York: Anchor, 1969.

Berger, Peter L., Brigitte Berger, and Hansfried Kellner. *The Homeless Mind: Modernization and Consciousness.* New York: Vintage Books, 1974.

Bergler, Thomas. *The Juvenilization of American Christianity.* Grand Rapids: Eerdmans, 2012.

Bowler, Kate. *Blessed: A History of the American Prosperity Gospel.* New York: Oxford University Press, 2013.

Brandi, Clara, and Max Buge. "A Cartography of the New Middle Classes in Developing and Emerging Countries." Deutsches Institut Für Entwicklungspolitik. Discussion Paper 35, 2014.

Brockington, Joseph L., and Judith Bahemuka, eds. *East Africa in Transition: Communities, Cultures, and Change.* Nairobi: Acton Publishers, 2004.

Cagnolo, C. *The Akikuyu: Their Customs, Traditions, and Folklore.* 1933. Reprint, Wisdom Graphics Place, 2006.

Chabal, Patrick. *Africa Works: Disorder as Political Instrument.* African Issues. Bloomington: Indiana University Press, 1999.

Charan, Ram, Stephen Drotter, and James Noel. *The Leadership Pipeline: How to Build the Leadership Powered Company.* San Francisco: Jossey-Bass, 2010.

Dorsett, Lyle W. *A Passion for Souls: The Life of D. L. Moody.* Chicago: Moody Publishers, 2003.

Freitas, Donna. *Sex and the Soul: Juggling Sexuality, Spirituality, Romance, and Religion on America's College Campuses.* New York: Oxford University Press, 2008.

Frykenberg, Robert Eric, and Alaine M. Low. *Christians and Missionaries in India: Cross-Cultural Communication Since 1500, with Special Reference to Caste, Conversion, and Colonialism.* Grand Rapids: Eerdmans, 2003.

Gi Hong, Young. "The Impact of Charismatic Pastoral Leadership on Religious Commitment and Church Growth in the Korean Mega-Churches." *Mission Studies* 18, no. 2036 (2001): 21-48.

Gifford, Paul. *Christianity, Politics, and Public Life in Kenya.* New York: Columbia University Press, 2009.

———. *Ghana's New Christianity: Pentecostalism in a Globalising African Economy.* London: Hurst & Co, 2004.

Green, Maia. *Priests, Witches, and Power: Popular Christianity After Mission in Southern Tanzania.* New York: Cambridge University Press, 2003.

Guinness, Os. *Dining with the Devil: The Megachurch Movement Flirts with Modernity.* Grand Rapids: Baker Books, 1993.

Hanciles, Jehu. *Beyond Christendom: Globalization, African Migration, and the Transformation of the West.* Maryknoll, NY: Orbis Books, 2009.

Hastings, Adrian. *The Church in Africa: 1450-1950.* Oxford History of the Christian Church. New York: Oxford University Press, 2004.

Hiebert, Paul G. *Understanding Folk Religion: A Christian Response to Popular Beliefs and Practices.* Grand Rapids: Baker Academic, 2000.

Hunter, James Davison. *To Change the World: The Irony, Tragedy, and Possibility of Christianity in the Late Modern World.* New York: Oxford University Press, 2010.

Hutchinson, Mark. *A Short History of Global Evangelicalism.* New York: Cambridge University Press, 2012.

James, Jonathan D., ed. *A Moving Faith: Mega Churches Go South.* Thousand Oaks, CA: Sage Publications, 2015.

Jinbong, Kim, P. Dwight Baker, and J. Nelson Jennings, eds. *Megachurch Accountability in Missions: Critical Assessment Through Global Case Studies.* Pasadena, CA: William Carey Library, 2016.

Kalu, Ogbu. *African Christianity: An African Story.* Perspectives on Gender Discourse. Pretoria: University of Pretoria, 2005.

———. *African Pentecostalism: An Introduction.* New York: Oxford University Press, 2008.

Katongole, Emmanuel. *The Sacrifice of Africa: A Political Theology for Africa.* Grand Rapids: Eerdmans, 2011.

Kidd, Thomas S. *George Whitefield: America's Spiritual Founding Father.* New Haven, CT: Yale University Press, 2014.

Kim, Kirsteen. "Ethereal Christianity: Reading Korean Mega-Church Websites." *Studies in World Christianity* 13, no. 3 (December 1, 2007): 208-24.

Loveland, Anne C., and Otis B. Wheeler. *From Meetinghouse to Megachurch: A Material and Cultural History.* Columbia: University of Missouri Press, 2003.

Maathai, Wangari. *The Challenge for Africa.* New York: Pantheon Books, 2009.

Marsh, Leslie L., and Hongmei Li. *The Middle Class in Emerging Societies: Consumers, Lifestyles, and Markets.* New York: Routledge, 2015.

McCandless, David. "The True Size of Africa." *Information Is Beautiful* (blog). October 14, 2010. http://informationisbeautiful.net/2010/the-true-size -of-africa/.

Meredith, Martin. *The State of Africa: A History of Fifty Years of Independence.* New York: Free Press, 2006.

Moyo, Dambisa, and Niall Ferguson. *Dead Aid: Why Aid Is Not Working and How There Is a Better Way for Africa.* New York: Farrar, Straus and Giroux, 2010.

Mugambi, Jesse Ndwiga Kanyua. *Christian Theology and Social Reconstruction.* Nairobi: Acton Publishers, 2003.

Netland, Harold A., and Craig Ott, eds. *Globalizing Theology: Belief and Practice in an Era of World Christianity.* Grand Rapids: Baker Academic, 2006.

Njogu, Kimani, and Garnette Oluoch-Olunya. *Cultural Production and Social Change in Kenya: Building Bridges.* Kenya: Twaweza Communications, 2007.

Noah, Trevor. *Born a Crime: Stories from a South African Childhood.* New York: Spiegel & Grau, 2016.

Noll, Mark A. *The Rise of Evangelicalism: The Age of Edwards, Whitefield and the Wesleys.* Downers Grove, IL: InterVarsity Press, 2010.

O'Malley, Steven, and Philomena Njeri Mwaura, eds. *African Urban Christian Identity: Emerging Patterns.* Nairobi: Acton Publishers, n.d.

Peterson, Eugene H. *Leap over a Wall: Earthy Spirituality for Everyday Christians.* San Francisco: HarperSanFrancisco, 1997.

Priest, Robert J., and Kirimi Barine, eds. *African Christian Leadership: Realities, Opportunities, and Impact.* Maryknoll, NY: Orbis Books, 2017.

Sachs, Jeffrey. *The End of Poverty: Economic Possibilities for Our Time.* New York: Penguin Press, 2005.

Sanneh, Lamin. *Disciples of All Nations: Pillars of World Christianity.* Oxford Studies in World Christianity. New York: Oxford University Press, 2008.

———. *Encountering the West: Christianity and the Global Cultural Process, the African Dimension.* World Christian Theology. Maryknoll, NY: Orbis Books 1993.

———. *Translating the Message: The Missionary Impact on Culture.* American Society of Missiology 13. Maryknoll, NY: Orbis Books, 1989.

Selasi, Taiye. "Bye-Bye Babar." *The LIP Magazine,* March 3, 2005. http://thelip .robertsharp.co.uk/?p=76.

Shaw, Mark. *Global Awakening: How 20th-Century Revivals Triggered a Christian Revolution.* Downers Grove, IL: IVP Academic, 2010.

———. *Work, Play, Love: A Visual Guide to Calling, Career, and the Mission of God.* Downers Grove, IL: InterVarsity Press, 2014.

Smith, Christian, Kari Christoffersen, Hilary Davidson, and Patricia Snell Herzog. *Lost in Transition: The Dark Side of Emerging Adulthood.* New York: Oxford University Press, 2011.

Smith, Christian, and Michael O. Emerson. *American Evangelicalism: Embattled and Thriving.* Chicago: University of Chicago Press, 1998.

Stanley, Brian. *The Bible and the Flag: Protestant Missions and British Imperialism in the Nineteenth and Twentieth Centuries.* Leicester, England: Apollos, 1990.

Stinton, Diane B., ed. *African Theology on the Way: Current Conversations.* SPCK International Study Guide 46. London: SPCK, 2010.

———. *Jesus of Africa: Voices of Contemporary African Christology.* Faith and Cultures. Maryknoll, NY: Orbis Books, 2004.

Thumma, Scott, and Dave Travis. *Beyond Megachurch Myths: What We Can Learn from America's Largest Churches.* San Francisco: Jossey-Bass, 2007.

Turner, Victor W. *The Ritual Process: Structure and Anti-Structure.* Chicago: Aldine, 1969.

United Nations. "United Nations Millennium Development Goals." Accessed May 24, 2016. www.un.org/millenniumgoals/.

———. "World Population Prospects: Key Findings." Department of Economic and Social Affairs, Population Division. Working Paper. ESA/P/WP 241 (2015).

———. "World Population Prospects: The 2010 Revision." Department of Economic and Social Affairs, Population Division. ST/ESA/SER.A/313 (2011). www.un.org/en/development/desa/population/publications/pdf/trends /WPP2010/WPP2010_Volume-I_Comprehensive-Tables.pdf.

Vaughan, John N. *The World's Twenty Largest Churches.* Grand Rapids: Baker Books, 1984.

Walls, Andrew. *The Cross-Cultural Process in Christian History: Studies in the Transmission and Appropriation of Faith.* Maryknoll, NY: Orbis Books, 2002.

———. *The Missionary Movement in Christian History: Studies in the Transmission of Faith.* Maryknoll, NY: Orbis Books, 1996.

Wandia, Njoya. "#LipaKamaTender Is No Longer a Strike; It's a Movement." *Love and Revolution* (blog). January 27, 2017. www.wandianjoya.com/1 /post/2017/01/lipakamatender-is-no-longer-a-strike-its-a-movement.html.

Wanjau, Muriithi. *Mizizi: Growing Deeper in Your Faith.* Nairobi: Clear Vision Media, 2005.

Wilson, Bryan R. *Religion in Sociological Perspective.* New York: Oxford University Press, 1982.

Woodberry, Robert D. "The Missionary Roots of Liberal Democracy." *American Political Science Review* 106, no. 2 (May 2012): 244-74.

World Bank. *Africa's Pulse: An Analysis of Issues Shaping Africa's Economic Future* 5 (April 2012).

Wrong, Michela. *It's Our Turn to Eat: The Story of a Kenyan Whistle-Blower.* New York: HarperCollins, 2010.

Wuthnow, Robert. *After the Baby Boomers: How Twenty- and Thirty-Somethings Are Shaping the Future of American Religion*. Princeton, NJ: Princeton University Press, 2007.

Wydick, Bruce, Paul Glewwe, and Laine Rutledge. "Does International Child Sponsorship Work? A Six-Country Study of Impacts on Adult Life Outcomes." *Journal of Political Economy* 121, no. 2 (April 1, 2013): 393-436. https://doi.org/10.1086/670138.

Young-Gi, Hong. "The Backgrounds and Characteristics of the Charismatic Mega-Churches in Korea." *Asia Journal of Pentecostal Studies* 3, no. 1 (2000): 99-118.

General Index

Scripture Index

MISSIOLOGICAL ENGAGEMENTS

Series Editors: Scott W. Sunquist, Amos Yong, and John R. Franke

Missiological Engagements: Church, Theology, and Culture in Global Contexts charts interdisciplinary and innovative trajectories in the history, theology, and practice of Christian mission at the beginning of the third millennium.

Among its guiding questions are the following: What are the major opportunities and challenges for Christian mission in the twenty-first century? How does the missionary impulse of the gospel reframe theology and hermeneutics within a global and intercultural context? What kind of missiological thinking ought to be retrieved and reappropriated for a dynamic global Christianity? What innovations in the theology and practice of mission are needed for a renewed and revitalized Christian witness in a postmodern, postcolonial, postsecular, and post-Christian world?

Books in the series, both monographs and edited collections, will feature contributions by leading thinkers representing evangelical, Protestant, Roman Catholic, and Orthodox traditions, who work within or across the range of biblical, historical, theological, and social-scientific disciplines. Authors and editors will include the full spectrum from younger and emerging researchers to established and renowned scholars, from the Euro-American West and the Majority World, whose missiological scholarship will bridge church, academy, and society.

Missiological Engagements reflects cutting-edge trends, research, and innovations in the field that will be of relevance to theorists and practitioners in churches, academic domains, mission organizations, and NGOs, among other arenas.

Finding the Textbook You Need

The IVP Academic Textbook Selector
is an online tool for instantly finding the IVP books
suitable for over 250 courses across 24 disciplines.

ivpacademic.com